Of Mind and Music

Of Mind and Music

LAIRD ADDIS

CORNELL UNIVERSITY PRESS

ITHACA AND LONDON

Copyright © 1999 by Cornell University

All rights reserved. Except for brief quotations in a review, this book, or parts thereof, must not be reproduced in any form without permission in writing from the publisher. For information, address Cornell University Press, Sage House, 512 East State Street, Ithaca, New York 14850.

First published 1999 by Cornell University Press.

Printed in the United States of America

Library of Congress Cataloging-in-Publication Data

Addis, Laird.
Of mind and music / Laird Addis.
p.   cm.
Includes bibliographical references (p.   ) and index.
ISBN 0-8014-3589-7 (alk. paper)
1. Music—Philosophy and aesthetics.   2. Music—Psychology.
ML3800.A37   1999
781.1′7—dc21   98-55442

Cornell University Press strives to use environmentally responsible suppliers and materials to the fullest extent possible in the publishing of its books. Such materials include vegetable-based, low-VOC inks and acid-free papers that are recycled, totally chlorine-free, or partly composed of nonwood fibers. Books that bear the logo of the FSC (Forest Stewardship Council) use paper taken from forests that have been inspected and certified as meeting the highest standards for environmental and social responsibility. For further information, visit our website at www.cornellpress.cornell.edu.

Cloth printing   10 9 8 7 6 5 4 3 2 1

FSC FSC Trademark © 1996 Forest Stewardship Council A.C.
SW-COC-098

To Patricia

*Love or music—which power can uplift man
to the sublimest heights? It is a large question;
yet it seems to me that one should answer it in
this way: Love cannot give an idea of music;
music can give an idea of love. But why
separate them? They are two wings of the soul.*

—Hector Berlioz

Contents

Contents

Preface

Many years ago, when I was an undergraduate student in music and before I began formal study of philosophy, I read Susanne Langer's *Philosophy in a New Key*. I had already been struck by the power of music, and so the book made a profound impression on me, for it seemed to contain a plausible account of why music is so important in the lives of so many people and of some importance in almost everyone's life. Considering myself a rational person who accepted a scientific worldview and who was opposed to mystery-mongering about any subject, I nevertheless felt a certain bewilderment as to why anyone who was so committed should have such an attraction to music.

It was still in my undergraduate years that I had the good fortune to hear a lecture by Leonard Meyer on the subject of emotion and music. This occasion enhanced my interest in the topic, and I have not forgotten the kindness and good humor with which he received my clumsily formulated questions at the end of his talk.

When, a few years later and by now a philosophy professor, I was asked to give some lectures on musical aesthetics to a group of high school music teachers on campus for the summer to pursue advanced degrees, I chose Langer's other major work in philosophy of art, *Feeling and Form*, as the textbook. Once again, I felt that this greatly underestimated philosopher (Susanne Katherina Knauth Langer, 1895–1985) had laid the foundations for an understanding of the nature and potency of music for human beings.

I recount these autobiographical details not because they have anything to do with the truth or plausibility of either Langer's theory or my own but as a way of acknowledging at the very beginning the single most important source for the reflections that follow. My theory is a development and extension of hers, different in detail and, more important, in scope and foundation, but would have been altogether impossible without her.

If Susanne Langer was the most important philosopher of music of a half century ago and Leonard Meyer of the next generation, Peter Kivy occupies that position in our own time. Over the last twenty years or so, Kivy has developed a powerful, subtle, and persuasive account of musical expression. Insofar as this account describes some of the ways in which the emotions are involved in music, one can only agree. But to the extent that it constitutes repudiation of the main features of a "representative" theory of music—Langer's or anyone else's—it will be disputed in the pages that follow. The reader will find, therefore, both enthusiastic endorsement and vehement disagreement with this or that of Kivy's ideas, as my own views dictate. I note here, and express my deep gratitude for, the assistance Peter Kivy has given me, in many ways, with the writing and publication of this book.

As its title indicates, this small book is a study in the philosophy of music *and* the philosophy of mind. While the questions about music that it tries to answer are very old ones and while some of the answers are themselves very old, the theory of the nature of music is embedded, as it were, in an ontology of mind in a way that is unlike, and more intimate than, any previous account. Indeed, if I may be so bold, no earlier account of the nature and appeal of music has invoked to a significant degree any explicit philosophy of mind. But then such *ontologies of mind*—which is what I mean by genuine philosophy of mind—are themselves exceedingly rare. Yet, if I am not mistaken, no philosophical account of what music is for human beings can be ultimate or adequate unless it contains or presupposes a plausible theory of the nature of the mind.

It might be objected that it is begging the question to suppose in advance that there is any such dependency of an adequate theory of music on an adequate theory of mind. To some extent I agree, but the fact is that in no previous account is it explained why *sounds* should be so significant for *consciousness*. This significance has been asserted, but the fundamental question of the bond between aural phenomenal and mental phenomena has not previously been answered or even really asked.

The main contribution of this study is to formulate and defend a theory about what might be called *the ontological affinity of mind and music*. Somewhat more precisely, it is sounds and conscious states that I assert to have the affinity, a kind of similarity that grounds the process whereby music *represents* to us certain emotions, moods, and other states of mind. That music somehow represents, or symbolizes, the emotions is an old theory, perhaps to be found even in Aristotle. It has remained to explain how sounds can accomplish this remarkable effect, and I hope to have taken some small step to that end.

Parts of this essay were read at the XIIIth International Congress of Aesthetics in Lahti, Finland, and the XIVth Congress of the International Association of Empirical Aesthetics in Prague, Czech Republic; at a symposium on the philosophy of music at a meeting of the American Philosophical Association in Pittsburgh; and at the Research Club, the Faculty Colloquium of the Department of Philosophy, and the Musicology Colloquium of the School of Music, all at the University of Iowa. Helpful comments and criticisms were made to me on all of these occasions.

I am grateful to my home institution, the University of Iowa, for giving me a semester of research leave during which time I wrote the first draft of this book. Permissions to reproduce the musical examples in this book have been received from the publishers of the scores from which they are taken.

LAIRD ADDIS

Iowa City, Iowa

OF MIND AND MUSIC

1

Music's Power

L et us begin with the fact that the employment of sounds, by way of production and audition, is common among many of the life forms of planet Earth and especially among a large family of animals of which our species is one. Whether or not organized in the ways that constitute what we call language, for most species sounds serve, whether or not by intention, as means of communicating various circumstances. These circumstances range from the presence of a predator (as indicated by the yelp of a prairie dog) to the quantum structure of the universe (as described in the speech of a physicist). Some of these sounds, in other species, we call the "songs" of birds and of whales. But even if it is only a matter of degree, our species stands distantly alone in the interest, the time, and the effort its members devote to producing, listening to, studying, and otherwise involving themselves in those sounds, and especially in those sounds we call music.

Why this unique interest in *sounds* on the part of *homo sapiens*? Although it is no doubt true that people enjoy music, it is superficial to say that humans listen to, create, facilitate, support, and otherwise advance the world of music because they like music. That amounts to little more, if any more, than saying that the human involvement in music is, for the most part, voluntary. If we accept the fact that humans like music as any kind of explanation for why they do music, we still want to ask why they like it.

One reason that the human involvement in music is puzzling is that, at one of the most important levels of looking at the question, it seems initially to admit either of no answer at all or else of one that would suggest that humans would *not* have much interest in music. For, from the evolutionary perspective, one would assume that an activity in which nearly every human takes part in one way or another and that has come to dominate the lives of a significant minority of many peoples must have a strong adaptive value, something that enhances the probability of survival, at least through the age of reproduction, and that thereby benefits the species itself. But what could that adaptive value be? And would finding such a benefit really explain how it is that humans involve themselves so much in the world of sounds?

It has been argued that music "functions," despite its now frequent character as a solitary activity, primarily as an activity (whether listening or performing) that enhances the solidarity of the community and that, like many other ritual activities, by increasing the probability of their occurrences, encourages those kinds of behaviors that in the biological sense benefit the individual and thereby also the species. If a greater sense of community with one's comrade listeners and performers of music from the listening and performing of music itself increases the probability that one will assist those comrades, in whatever way that has the requisite biological consequences, then the evolutionary mandate that major behaviors of a species must have, at least originally, some adaptive value has been satisfied.

At the same time, it might be argued that an activity that takes so much time from those pursuits that have more directly to do with biological survival can only very indirectly be understood by way of natural selection and that in any case some further explanation is needed. The point here is not to cast any doubt on the methodological assumptions or procedures, much less the findings, of evolutionary biology but to insist that it cannot possibly provide a complete answer to our puzzle about the human involvement in music. But this argument has barely begun.

Sigmund Freud, from a perspective similar to that of evolutionary biology, also found the human interest in music and the other arts initially problematic. What, he wondered, is the connection between this major aspect of human existence and that impulse that is essential to the continuation of the species and that is, according to him, the fundamental impulse, overtly or covertly, in most of the activities of our daily lives?

Insisting that expression of the sexual impulse and others that he believed to be innate to the species must be inhibited and even prohibited if we are also to be able to engage in the other activities that are essential to our survival, especially the activities that require cooperative behavior, Freud theorized that the arts as well as the pleasures of jokes and the illusions of religions and ideologies assist humans in what he called, somewhat hyperbolically on his own theories, the "renunciation of the instincts." Involvement in the arts, including music, serves to mitigate the effects on the individual of the inherent and ineradicable conflict between the desires of the individual on the one hand and the demands of social existence on the other, or as internalized by the individual, the struggle between the id and the superego. Art somehow strengthens the side of the superego; not, as in the case of religions and ideologies, by enlisting the gods or the trends of history as its advocates thus constraining the otherwise reluctant individual with threats of punishment or promises of reward, but by directly enhancing the sense of social solidarity.

Granted that participation in the arts, including music, strengthens social solidarity and so has adaptive benefit as seen from both the evolutionary and the Freudian points of view (which, properly understood, are complementary and not contrary to one another), it must be insisted also that the solidarity that is strengthened is rarely with the species as a whole. If there sometimes seems to be contradiction between those who, on the one hand, innocently proclaim that music refines the person and makes us better world citizens (while perhaps also describing music as "the universal language") and those who, on the other hand, understand the power of music in many cases to heighten the hatred of the (also human) adversary and to reinforce determination, perhaps in physical battle, to defeat the enemy, one need only remember that the community that is strengthened, the solidarity that is enhanced, the allegiance that is intensified, the renunciation that is accomplished, is always greatest with respect to the group or groups to which one's ties are strongest. And such ties are, if we be honest about it, not usually those of our professed and not wholly inefficacious values; they are instead those of our deepest emotions. But evolutionary theory does not preclude struggles between groups within the species; indeed it often sees struggle as being to the overall, long-term benefit of the species.

Music, however, remains a special case. To speak merely of the anthropological facts, music alone among the arts is universal in the precise sense that almost literally every human being who has the perceptual and mental capacities to do so listens to music; and—what is not quite the same fact—by any reasonable measure, the creation, performance, hearing, and study of music occupy more time and absorb more resources in most cultures than all of the other arts put together. What accounts for the *special* appeal of music among the various arts? Why should the perception of certain kinds of *sounds* have the profound effect it apparently does have on behaviors that seem to have nothing to do with anything aural? Is there something peculiar to the nature of sound with respect to the organs of perception or the nature of human awareness that gives sound its special importance as compared even with the data of vision in the human involvement in the arts? Why, to return to an earlier formulation, do we so much "like" music?

Having construed the question in this way, some people may be tempted to say that that's just the way things are with people and music: there is, it will be said, a law of nature that organisms of a certain kind when subject to sounds of a certain kind will be more likely to behave in certain ways than if they were not subject to those sounds; and because those behaviors are generally beneficial to the species, evolutionary pressures have taken advantage of the mutations that produce pleasure in hearing such sounds. Furthermore, this law, it may be added, while probably reducible to more basic laws at the molecular level about cells and sound waves, is not further explainable in any interesting way at the level of the organism by way of the nature of what is *perceived by* or *represented to* or *brought to mind in* the listeners of music. At the level of the organism and its mental states, there is really nothing more to say, according to this account, than that a certain "stimulus" produces, or tends to produce, a certain "response" in organisms of a certain kind.

We need not doubt the existence of some such law about humans and sounds or its reducibility to laws about the micro-world in order to insist that its purported *ultimate* explanation of the power of music in human affairs is really only a slightly more "scientific" way of restating, instead of explaining, the truism that people listen to music because they want to. And while the reality *could* have been such that an explanation of this kind be, at that level, the ultimate one about people and sounds (much as, it would seem, analogous laws about the universal aspects of human likes and dislikes in tastes or colors are ultimate), we know very well, when we think about it, that much more is involved in the case of music.

The empirical absurdity of treating the relation between human beings and music as *mere* "stimulus/response" is attested to, or at least
strongly supported by, numerous facts, among them that most pieces
of music involve consciously constructed structures of a certain sort,
which structures are more or less perceived by listeners; that listening
to some music requires effort and attention and memory of sorts that
may be reasonably be called *cognitive*; that the pleasures of music are,
while sometimes also physical, for the most part of a sort difficult to
characterize or categorize, but that surely involve the *appreciation* of
certain, often complex properties of the music one is hearing and perhaps also a measure of pride in being able to discern or otherwise know
or understand certain properties of the music; and that in talking about
music, we use the language of the emotions and other aspects of mental life to characterize the music itself.

For anyone who is familiar with the relevant literature, a more general
fact of which the last-mentioned above is an aspect will be recognized
as the one most often called attention to and discussed when one is considering the power of music in human affairs; namely, the vague fact of
the connection of music and emotion. One reason for our making this
connection derives, indubitably, from the relation between the notions
of "power" and "emotion" themselves; for what can "move" us ('motion' and 'emotion' having strongly shared etymologies) has force. But
just as indubitably, the primary reason comes from the anthropological
fact that when humans *talk about* music, they almost invariably use the
language of emotion to do so. This fact needs no documentation, for it
is known to anyone who attends even slightly to the relevant acts of
speech or inscription. No doubt there is some connection between these
two crucial facts—that music affects our emotions and that we use the
language of emotion to describe music—but what that connection is, or
might be, must await further investigation.

So we are led to the idea, from which I might have chosen to start, that
the heart of the explanation of why humans like music, why they give
so much of their time and money and labor to music, has to do with
some important connection or connections between music and their
emotions. And while one may reasonably surmise, what I am inclined
to believe, that the realm of mental life that is "expressed" by music is
broader than that of the emotions alone, we may continue here by categorizing and outlining the major theories as to the nature of the connection between music and the emotions. More precisely, we should

say that these are theories about what the most important or *fundamental* connection is: one might hold (as I believe one should hold) that while there is one most important connection, music "expresses" the emotions and other mental states in several, perhaps many, ways, no one of which renders impossible any other that is recognized by extant theories.

Music, we say easily and naturally, *expresses* emotion. Music is sad or joyful, angry or moody, and so on. As it happens, the notion of expression has sometimes been appropriated for special theoretical purposes, and some musicians—most famously Eduard Hanslick among theorists—are said to have denied that music expresses anything. I shall try to take the words 'music expresses emotion' as a theory-neutral way of referring to what, Hanslick and others possibly notwithstanding, I take to be a *datum*, that is, that there is some important connection, whatever it is, between music and the emotions, one result of which is the anthropological fact mentioned above. I suggest that Hanslick and others, in their remarks against expression in music, were not really denying the datum but instead rejecting certain theories about the datum. In the cases of certain twentieth-century composers, they were, in their words as in their music, reacting to Romantic excesses of theory and compositional practice. Denying that there is any important connection between music and the emotions is absurd on both anthropological and phenomenological grounds (the phenomenological itself underlying the anthropological); and if Hanslick or anyone else really is to be convicted of this absurdity, so be it.[1]

What, then, are the theories of the connection between music and the emotions, the formulation and defense of one such theory being the burden of this essay? No doubt there are many serviceable ways of categorizing the theories, but I find the following way the best for my purposes, stated for clarity of exposition as if there were, contrary to almost certain fact, only one connection between music and the emotions.

It is to be kept in mind, with respect to all the theories about the connection of music and the emotions, that in the literal sense an emotion is something that is felt or had or thought about only by a sentient being. This way of putting this fact is not to endorse any particular theory

---

[1] For Hanslick's treatment of expression in music, see his *The Beautiful in Music*, trans. Gustav Cohen (New York: Liberal Arts Press, 1957).

about the nature of emotion but only to remind ourselves of the commonsense fact, recognized by all extant theories, that in no case is the sadness of a piece of music to be understood as the music's feeling sad or being in mind of sadness. To feel sadness or to think about sadness can be properties only of a conscious being, and music is not a conscious being. And it will be well also to fix in our minds the distinction I have just been invoking—that between *having* an emotion and only *being in mind of* an emotion. It is obvious that one can *think about* sadness without *feeling* sad (as I hope you, the reader, are doing as you grasp these words) and so for all the emotions, just as one can think about being sweaty or being magnetic without feeling or being sweaty or magnetic.

I want now to elucidate five theories as to what kinds of facts are fundamentally involved in the possession by music of features that lead humans to characterize music in the language of emotion. Every such theory is either a *causal* theory or else an *inherence* theory.

A causal theory of emotion in music is one that maintains that the application of the predicates of emotion to music should be understood *either* by way of how the music came about, that is, what caused it, *or* by way of its effects, that is, what it causes or would cause in the listener. What are not relevant are the natures of the properties of the music itself except, of course, for their causal powers. The first of these causal theories, generally associated with Romanticism and the cult of the individual musician (whether composer, conductor, or performer) and what I shall call the *composer-causal theory*, holds that the emotional qualities of a piece of music are to be understood as expressions of the composer's feelings. Thus, on the composer-causal theory, it will be said that, *because* Ernst Krenek felt grief when he wrote his *Symphonic Elegy* shortly after the death of, and in memory of, his friend Anton Webern, the passage beginning in measure 100 of Example 1, from among many examples in the piece one could have chosen, expresses grief.

On the composer-causal view, just as a person in daily life expresses emotion through bodily movements and positions and through facial expressions so that, in one sense at least, a sad face is in its sadness one caused by the sadness of the person with the face, so a sad piece of music is an outward expression of, by way of being caused by, a person who either feels sad or who, according to a weaker version of the theory, is in mind of sadness. One wants to distinguish, to be sure, between composing a piece of music as a causal consequence (perhaps unknown

Example 1. Ernst Krenek, measures 84–110, *Symphonic Elegy for String Orchestra*
© 1947 Elkan-Vogel, Inc. Used by permission.

to the composer) of the composer's state of mind and composing a piece of music as the intentional expression of the composer's state of mind. But either way, on the composer-causal view, just as one must know that the person feels sad in order to be certain that this really is a sad face (and not just a sad-*looking* face, as in a Saint Bernard dog), so one must know, it would seem, that the composer really felt sad, or at least was in mind of sadness, in order to be certain that this is a sad piece of music.

The other form of a causal theory of the emotions in music calls attention not to its causes but instead to its effects; specifically, to its effects on actual or ideal listeners to the music. (The distinction between the actual and the ideal listener is important to some theorists, and invoking

Example 2. Ludwig von Beethoven, Marcia Funebre movement, measures 1–9, *Symphony No. 3*

ideal instead of actual listeners or viewers or readers is a device used in many aesthetic theories for making them more plausible.) According to this form of a causal theory, which I shall call the *listener-causal theory*, a sad piece of music is one that causes sadness or the thought of sadness in the listener. Thus the listener-causal theory holds that, *because* most people feel sad or are put in mind of sadness when they hear the passage of Example 2, among many such passages in the Marcia Funebre movement of Ludwig von Beethoven's *Symphony No. 3*, the passage expresses sadness.

The listener-causal theory is, in an important way, closer to inherence theories of emotion in music than to the composer-causal theory, and discussion of this point will both provide an introduction to discussion of inherence theories and give us initial acquaintance with a subtle but vitally important distinction for understanding the issues before us.

The composer-causal theory, according to which the sadness of the music derives from, really just is, the fact that the composer felt or thought of sadness and perhaps intended, whether successfully or not, that the music express sadness, does not require that the music have any *specific* intrinsic properties whatsoever. All that is required is that certain events have taken place in the mind of the composer by way of having certain feelings, thoughts, and intentions. The listener-causal theory, by contrast, does require that the music have the specific intrinsic properties necessary to cause certain feelings or thoughts in the listener. Such properties of the music itself—that is, intrinsic to it—may or may not be perceptible properties that the listener is able consciously to grasp or to attend to, but in any case they must be, or also be, *dispositional* properties of the music. Thus the listener-causal theory of emotion in music does require the music to have certain specific intrinsic properties.

But it is very important to understand, if the purely causal aspect of the listener-causal theory is to be retained and the theory thereby distinguished from inherence theories, that those intrinsic properties of the music that do cause certain feelings or thoughts in the listener could be or, better put, *could have been* any properties whatsoever that music might possess. For on the listener-causal theory, music is like a sadness pill; and just as the pill taker need not perceive or even know or have any idea of what intrinsic property of the pill is responsible for the subsequent sadness, while it is in an overall sense the listening to the music that causes sadness or the thought of sadness in the listener, the specific properties of the music that are causally responsible for the effect in the listener may or may not be perceived as such or known or even understood by the listener. It might be, or *might have been*, any property whatsoever of the music. If the nature of the property itself is involved in any but a purely causal way, then, as I use the words, we no longer have a causal theory of emotion in music but some kind of inherence theory.

Causal theories of emotion in music—whether composer- or listener-causal—no longer find much favor with philosophers, and rightly so. I do not propose to rehearse the arguments against them here, nor do I have anything really new to add to those arguments. But I will note that in their common feature of denying that what gives a piece or passage of music whatever emotional character it has is an inherent, perceptible property of a certain nature in the music itself, these theories seem to challenge not only the fundamental experience of music listeners but also the reports of many composers themselves. That, of course, does not conclusively prove all such theories to be false, and it remains the case that many musicians easily fall into one causal theory or the other (or sometimes both!) in the way they talk about music. Performers and conductors are especially prone to the idea that what they are doing is "expressing" themselves in performing music as are composers in writing music, and of course these musicians are entirely correct at least to the extent that whatever a person does is some kind of expression of that person's feelings, thoughts, intentions, and other mental characteristics. From this undeniable fact, these musicians often move effortlessly to the conclusion that the emotional qualities of the music itself are not only due to them the musicians, which again is unquestionably true, but just *are* what goes on in the minds of the musicians. Music theorists and historians, on the other hand, seem to incline more to the other form of causal theory, perhaps being both more skeptical of the reality and the power of what goes on in the minds of their composing and performing colleagues as well as more knowledgeable of the fads and ideologies of the moment, with their emphases on listener's or viewer's or reader's responses, possibly as a means of "challenging authority" or of "democratizing the arts." Let us move on to inherence theories.

An inherence theory of emotion in music is one that maintains that the application of the predicates of emotion to music should be understood by way of the *natures* of some of the properties of the music itself and therefore independently of how the music came about or its mere causal powers. While the causal connection between the music performed and the aural perception of it obviously must be a part of any theory about the connection of emotion and music, inherence theories, in contrast to causal theories, insist that attention must be given to the natures of some of the properties of music themselves and not only their place in some causal sequence of composition, performance, and hearing. In its emotional aspects, according to these theories, a piece of music is not either *merely* an outward expression of its composer's feeling or *merely* the contingent cause of some feelings or thoughts of such feelings in the listener.

There are three kinds of inherence theories: what I will call the *pure-inherence theory*, the *resemblance-inherence theory*, and the *intentional-inherence theory*. The latter two theories may both also be called forms of *representative-inherence theories*, for on both of them, the emotional content of music is to be understood as involving some kind of (noncausal) connection—resemblance or intentional—of certain properties of music to the emotions or some aspect of the emotions of a sort that may, broadly, be said to be that of representing the emotions. Yet, because the natures of those properties of music are essential to how and what they represent, they are, as I use the words, forms of inherence theories along with the pure inherence theory. Let us consider each kind in more detail.

The pure-inherence theory may be stated as follows: music has certain objective properties that can be described in purely acoustical terms such as pitch, duration, timbre, and so on. But some of these properties, or complexes of them, may reasonably also be called *expressive* properties because the perception of them in their intrinsic natures puts the listener in mind of certain emotions. So, on the pure-inherence theory, it will be said that the acoustical properties of the sounds in the passage of Example 3 from the Adagio of Gustav Mahler's *Symphony No. 9* just are the expressive property of anguish.

However, and this is the crucial point, there is nothing interesting to be said about any connection between the relevant properties of the music and the emotions themselves that are brought to mind in the listener; at the same time, it *is* the inherent natures of the musical properties perceived as expressive properties that are relevant and not just their causal powers. The lack of significant or systematic connection is what makes it a "pure" inherence theory; the insistence on the importance of the natures of the relevant properties is what makes it an inherence theory.

A representative theory, whether one of resemblance or of intentionality, is one that does rely on some kind of significant connection between the inherent natures of the properties of the music and the emotions. But before I say more carefully what each kind of theory involves, it will be worthwhile asking whether or not the pure-inherence theory is really intelligible in the sense of being able to find a place between, on the one side, the listener-causal theory and, on the other, some form of representative theory. The listener-causal theory says it is just the causal powers of the music that are relevant whatever the inherent natures of

Example 3. Gustav Mahler, Adagio movement, measures 1–15, *Symphony No. 9*
Vienna: Universal-Edition, 1912, republication © 1993 by Dover Publications, Inc.
Used by permission.

the properties of the music, while representative theories say it is the inherent natures of the properties as they stand in some important systematic connection to the emotions that explain emotion in music. The pure-inherence theory seems to want to have it both ways in insisting on the importance of the inherent natures of the properties of music while denying that they have any systematic connection to emotions themselves. Is this really a possibly true theory?

Had not so distinguished a philosopher of music as Peter Kivy set out and defended what appears to me to be just this theory in his *Music Alone*, probably I should myself not have been able to make the distinctions, or apparent distinctions, that drive my categorization of the five theories and to isolate the pure-inherence theory as a distinct theory.[2] In

---

2   Peter Kivy, *Music Alone: Philosophical Reflections on the Purely Musical Experience* (Ithaca: Cornell University Press, 1990), especially chapter 9, "Hearing the Emotions." It is possible, but not obvious, that something like the pure-inherence theory can also be found in the writings of Victor Zuckerhandl. For example, in distinguishing his views from those of Susanne Langer, he states his own in this way: "tones are not primarily something

fact, Kivy is, or has been, best known for defending a form of representative theory, and the pure-inherence theory (my name, not his) is intended, as I understand it, as a supplement to, and not a replacement for, the representative theory of *The Corded Shell* of a decade earlier.[3] That is, Kivy came to be increasingly impressed by music that, while having expressive qualities, seemed not very well to fit his form of a representative theory of the emotions to music. Be all that as it may, I observe here for later discussion that the pure-inherence theory would seem to be somewhat unstable, tending to fall either into the listener-causal theory or, more likely, a representative theory. For one wants to know just how it is that the properties perceived in the inherent natures by the listener can bring certain emotions to mind in any kind of systematic way if there is no relevant, intrinsic connection of those musical properties to the emotions. Let us look more closely at representative theories.

Representative theories of the connection between music and the emotions, we recall, divide between the resemblance-inherence theory and the intentionality-inherence theory. Broadly speaking, resemblance theories rely on some putative *similarity* between certain properties of music and certain properties "involved" in the emotions, while intentionality theories stress the idea that musical properties are *symbols* of certain properties "involved" in the emotions. In their actual, historical formulations the distinction is not so clear, resemblance theories also sometimes being called or being some form of "symbolic" theories, and intentionality theories sometimes involving resemblance to some degree. Still, I think the distinction is genuine and useful, and will proceed accordingly. As to the properties of the emotions that are represented, we have a further complication.

---

external related to some inner life; the relationship between external and internal is wholly embedded in the tone itself. The inner life which music reveals behind the external tones is the inner life of the tones themselves, not that of a psyche. . . . The musical tone is symbolic not because it helps us to perceive something that is in principle unperceivable, but primarily because its pure dynamism is directly apprehended by the ear. In so far as it can be called 'expression,' it is not expression of a feeling, but of the tone's own dynamic quality." Victor Zuckerhandl, *Sound and Symbol: Music and the External World*, trans. Willard R. Trask (New York: Pantheon, 1956), 153–154.

3 Peter Kivy, *The Corded Shell: Reflections on Musical Expression* (Princeton: Princeton University Press, 1980). But it may be usefully and in fairness added that since his *Music Alone*, Kivy has become even more skeptical, perhaps fully so, of any kind of representative theory. See Peter Kivy, *Philosophies of Art: An Essay in Differences* (Cambridge: Cambridge University Press, 1997), especially the chapter called "The Liberation of Music."

There are the emotions themselves, the physiological accompaniments to the emotions, and the behavioral expressions of the emotions.[4] Some representative theories hold that what is represented by music is not the emotions themselves but instead the inward, felt physiological accompaniments of the emotions in human beings, while others hold that it is the outward, observable behavioral expressions of the emotions in human beings. Mixing the two categories, we may say that according to such theories it is certain bodily motions, facial expressions, linguistic acts, heartbeat rates, muscular tensions, and so on that certain properties of music can and do represent. Even more succinctly, we may say that it is the *physical* expression of emotion, whether physiological or behavioral, that is directly represented by music, taking for granted the listener's knowledge of the connections between such physical expressions and the emotions themselves. The reader may suspect —correctly—that resemblance theories are somewhat more likely than intentional theories to affirm that it is the physical expression of emotion and not emotion itself that is directly represented by music. For it is, at least initially, more plausible to maintain that some properties of music are more similar to certain physical properties of human beings than to the mental properties of the emotions themselves. Thus, according to the resemblance-inherence theory, it will be said that in the passage of Example 4 from Aaron Copland's *Four Dances from Rodeo*, the fast and snappy meter *resembles* the fast gait of an exuberant person, the awareness of which similarity brings to mind exuberance in the listener.

But whether the nonmusical *relata* of the resemblance relation are supposed to be the emotions themselves or only their physical expression, the relation itself is intrinsic in the sense that it is, so to speak, in nature itself and not one that is culturally determined or otherwise conventional. It can be granted that the resemblances we notice are in part a matter of culture; but if the resemblance-inherence theory is to have any power, it is essential to insist on the "natural" character of the relation of resemblance. If it is asked how, given the symmetry of the relation of resemblance, the music manages to represent the emotions or their

---

[4] Many philosophers, possibly including Susanne Langer, would deny that there are such things as "the emotions themselves" distinct from their physiological and behavioral aspects. This important question of the ontology of the emotions cannot be argued here; I take for granted, rightly or wrongly, the commonsense view that an emotion is a "feeling" over and above its physiological accompaniments and behavioral expressions, and that therefore these philosophers are mistaken. But I have provided reasons for what is here taken for granted in Laird Addis, "The Ontology of Emotion," *Southern Journal of Philosophy* 33 (1995): 261–278.

Example 4. Aaron Copland, Four Dance Episodes, measures 1–6, from "Buckaroo Holiday," *Rodeo*

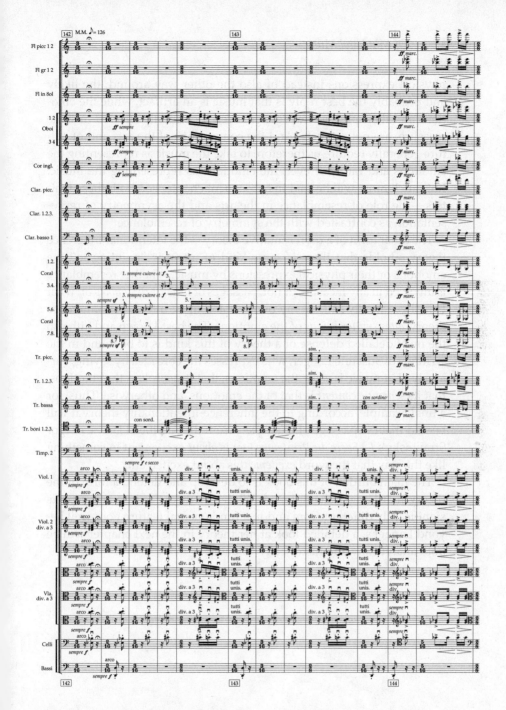

Example 5. Igor Stravinsky, Sacrificial Dance movement, measures 1–12, *Le Sacré du Printemps*.

physical expressions instead of also the other way around, the likely and probably the best reply is that music is an artifact, while the emotions and their physical expression, even if culturally affected in some measure, are not artifacts. And the conventions of the arts and of culture generally require us therefore to take the music as representing the emotions and rarely, if ever, the emotions as representing the music. But much more will be said in subsequent chapters on both these matters—the role of resemblance in the arts and the asymmetry of representation as contrasted with the symmetry of resemblance.

The other form of a representative theory—the intentional-inherence theory—holds that there is some kind of intrinsic "pointing to" the emotions or their physical expressions by music. Whether resemblance is involved in any measure or not, passages of music are *symbols* or, what I shall eventually call, on my own version of an intentional-inherence theory, *quasi-natural signs* of the emotions. The best-known and hitherto the most detailed defense of a theory of this kind is to be found in the writings of Susanne Langer, who expresses the core idea by saying, variously, that music is *about* the emotions, that it *symbolizes* the emotions, that its *semantic content* is that of the emotions, and otherwise. Thus, for a final example, according to the inherence-intentionality theory it will be said that the passage of Example 5 from the Sacrificial Dance of Igor Stravinsky's *Le Sacre du Printemps* just is *about* excitement in something like the way that the word *excitement* is about excitement.

The main burden of this book is to develop and defend a form of the theory that Langer championed. While my theory is in many aspects significantly different from and in a fundamental feature goes well beyond Langer's, a detailed look at her theory in the next chapter will be both analytically and historically valuable.

2

Langer's Theory

The idea that music, more than simply sometimes putting listeners in mind of emotions, somehow "naturally" represents the emotions does not, probably needless to say, originate with Susanne Langer. She herself cites numerous philosophers, psychologists, and musicians (including Schopenhauer and Wagner) among her predecessors. She does not mention some of the more interesting philosophers who held some such view, from Aristotle and Boethius among the ancients to, in the eighteenth century, Condillac, Diderot, and Rousseau—some of whom even wrote of music as a "natural sign" of the emotions. And while, like so many others, these thinkers frequently confused the idea of emotions as *represented* by music with the idea of the emotions as *expressed* by music (in the sense of what the composer felt or had in mind) or the idea of the emotions as *aroused* by music, nonetheless their works contain the core idea of a direct, intrinsic connection between music and the emotions of a sort such that the former is *about* the latter. In the chapters that follow I will have more to say about the notion of a "natural sign" and its applicability to music.

Langer's theory of music and the emotions, although not embedded in an explicit ontology of mind, is positioned within broader philosophical theories: on the one hand, a general theory of signs and symbols that is intended to apply to language proper as well as to music and elsewhere, and, on the other hand, a theory of the arts that includes many aspects unrelated directly to matters of representation but that nevertheless centers on the notion of "significance" in the arts. (The key chapter of the primary source for her philosophy of music, *Philosophy in a New Key*, is titled "On Significance in Music."[1]) Fortunately, if I am not mistaken, we may for the most part safely ignore these broader theories for our purposes, the theory of music and the emotions being neither entailed by nor entailing those theories, although possibly gaining some overall plausibility from them to the extent that they are independently defensible.

The main component theses of Langer's theory may be stated succinctly as follows: (1) There is an *isomorphism* between music and the emotions. (2) There is a relation of *representation* by music of the emotions. (3) There is an *ineffability* in what music represents. Even without further detail as to the precise meanings of these three propositions, we can probably see, at least in the abstract, that they are logically independent theses. For isomorphisms can and do exist without any involvement of representation or ineffability, as in, for example, the isomorphisms that exist between any of various pairs of number series. Similarly, there can be representation without isomorphism as in the case of language itself, unless, as sometimes may be useful, 'isomorphism' is used so broadly that any kind of coordination or connection is an isomorphism, in which case, to be sure, all representation presupposes isomorphism. And ineffability, understood as the thesis that there are certain features of reality that no language can fully express, obviously does not imply that some other kind of representational system can do what language cannot or even that there are other representational systems.

The notion of isomorphism has, it seems, two distinct senses, although one of them may be, in a significant sense, reducible to the other. In the first place, there is the idea of one-to-one correspondence in the sense of there being a rule that generates a systematic correlation of the elements of one realm or domain to the elements of another. It is in this sense that the domain of all the positive integers is isomorphic to the domain of the even positive integers. But isomorphism can also be similarity or identity of *structure*, which may or may not permit one-to-one correlation, as in cases of convergent evolution such as that of whales and fishes; for here it is the *form* of the elements of the domains and not

---

[1]   Susanne Langer, *Philosophy in a New Key: A Study in the Symbolism of Reason, Rite, and Art*, 3d ed. (Cambridge: Harvard University Press, 1951); *PNK* in the text.

their *content* that is relevant; and different elements within a domain may have similar or identical form, differing only in content.

Needless to say, the notions of form and content are themselves somewhat obscure in the abstract, but it is this notion of similarity or identity of form that is relevant to the understanding of Langer's theory of the relation of music to the emotions. Thus she tells us that "musical structures logically resemble certain dynamic patterns of human experience" (*PNK*, 226), that "certain aspects of the so-called 'inner life' . . . have formal properties similar to those of music" (*PNK*, 228), and again, in her later *Feeling and Form*, that music and emotion have "some common logical form" such that music is "a tonal analogue of emotive life."[2]

So we are to understand that there is a similarity or identity of form between music and the emotions. But what *is* the form of a piece of music and, much more important, what *is* the form of an emotion? As for the forms of music, we may safely say that they are something that can be described fully in purely acoustical and temporal properties of the music—pitches, timbres, intervals, volumes, and so on along with durations and the relations of succession and simultaneity. But what about the forms of the emotions? How, and in what sense, does an emotion have a form? Langer's theory has come under attack for failing to elaborate sufficiently on this idea. What she actually says about the forms of the emotions amounts to listing the "formal properties" that emotion is said to share with music: "patterns of motion and rest, of tension and release, of agreement and disagreement, preparation, fulfillment, excitation, sudden change, etc." (*PNK*, 228). In *Feeling and Form*, her other important work devoted to philosophy of the arts, it is put not much differently (the relevant pages of this work being intended as a summary of the main theory of the earlier work):

> The tonal structures we call "music" bear a close logical similarity to the forms of human feeling—forms of growth and of attenuation, flowing and stowing, conflict and resolution, speed, arrest, terrific excitement, calm, or subtle activation and dreamy lapses—not joy and sorrow perhaps, but the poignancy of either and both—the greatness and brevity and eternal passing of everything vitally felt. Such is the pattern, or logical form, of sentience; and the pattern of music is that same form worked out in pure, measured sound and silence. (*FF*, 27)

---

[2] Susanne Langer, *Feeling and Form: A Theory of Art* (New York: Charles Scribner's Sons, 1953), 27; *FF* in the text.

On Langer's theory, partly because of the shared logical form between music and the emotions, music can also *represent* or, as she usually puts it, *symbolize* the emotions. (The notion of "logical form" comes from the work of Bertrand Russell, Ludwig Wittgenstein, and Rudolf Carnap—sources acknowledged by Langer—but with respect to what is said to be shared by propositions and facts, not music and emotions.) What, we must ask, is the relation of symbolizing, given the symmetry of shared logical form as against the asymmetry of the representing or symbolizing relation? As I have noted, some domains with shared logical form (that is, similarity or identity of structure) do not involve representation to any degree; and where there is representation, shared logical form alone clearly cannot determine which domain it is whose elements are represented and which whose elements represent. Langer has been accused, falsely, of supposing that the presumed shared logical form of music and the emotions is a *sufficient* condition for music's representing the emotions and not the other way around. What, then, does she take the further condition or conditions to be that ground the asymmetry of the representing or symbolizing relation in the case of music and the emotions?

In answering this question, we will do well to refer to Langer's broader theory of symbolism, which, she insists, is derived from the theories of Wittgenstein's *Tractatus Logico-Philosophicus*. Symbols, she says, are *"vehicles for the conception of objects"* adding somewhat confusingly that *"it is the conceptions, not the things, that symbols directly 'mean'"* (PNK, 60–61). By this she intends to distinguish symbols from *signs*, which, in her meaning, are used to provoke *actions*: "signs *announce* their objects to him [the listening subject], whereas symbols *lead him to conceive* their objects" (PNK, 61). Distinguishing between the "discursive" symbolism of language proper and the nondiscursive or "presentational" symbolism of nonlinguistic representational systems, she regards music, above all other symbolisms, as a nondiscursive representational system capable of symbolizing certain kinds of nonmusical features of reality, just because music is, in her judgment, "the most highly developed type of such purely connotational semantic" (PNK, 101). Although music "means" the *conceptions* of the emotions and symbolizes those emotions whose conceptions are "meant," music should not be said to *denote* either the emotions themselves or the conceptions of them. This is because, in her use, denotation implies constancy of reference of the elements of the symbolic system, a feature that is possessed by language but not by music, whose elements, taken singly, don't refer at all. Still, the distinction between denotative and nondenotative symbolisms is somewhat blurred in what amounts to Langer's explicit argument that music at least *can* be, while, by implication, the emotions themselves *cannot* be, a symbolic system:

> . . . there is no doubt that musical forms have certain properties to recommend them for symbolic use: they are composed of many separable items, easily produced, and easily combined in a great variety of ways; in themselves they play no important practical role which would overshadow their semantic function; they are readily distinguished, remembered, and repeated; and finally, they have a remarkable tendency *to modify each other's character in combination,* as words do, by all serving each as a context. The purely structural requirements for a symbolism are satisfied by the peculiar tonal phenomenon we call "music." (*PNK,* 228)

But there is another factor that is essential to this account. What the considerations so far mentioned establish at most is that music *can* and the emotions *cannot* symbolize; but many domains, from tinker toys to quilt patches, have elements that satisfy most of the characteristic conditions of symbolisms without actually being symbolisms. Although Langer doesn't present the factor explicitly as being vitally important to her conclusion that music not merely can but actually does symbolize the emotions, it is clear from a careful reading of *Philosophy in a New Key* that the additional factor is that of certain thoughts or mental dispositions of those who participate in the world of music; specifically, the *intentions* of composers and what we may call the *regardings* of listeners. That is, the composer intends that the music will symbolize certain mental phenomena, and the listener regards it as so symbolizing, at least in the ideal case. And it is important for us to see that the problem and the solution with which Langer is dealing are quite general ones. For one may well ask in the case of language proper how it is that it represents the nonlinguistic reality (and nonreality) and, even more fundamentally, how thoughts themselves are about whatever they are about. How, in any case we can imagine, do the elements of one kind of domain manage to *represent* those of another? I give much attention to this question (and its different answers in different kinds of cases) in the next chapter. But there is more yet to be said about Langer's specific answer to the question of what it is that makes it possible or even necessary that music represent the emotions.

Raising the issue again in *Feeling and Form*, Langer gives a somewhat different answer to the question with a seemingly greater emphasis on the role of choice, intention, and interest. Writing of a "motive for choosing" which domain will symbolize which, she tells us that "the decisive reason is that one [entity or system] is easier to perceive and handle than the other" and that "sounds are much easier to produce, combine, perceive, and identify, than feelings" (*FF*, 27). But further (perhaps combining what I called intentions and regardings into a single notion), Langer observes that "a symbol is used to articulate ideas of something we wish to think about. . . . So *interest* always plays a major part in making one thing, or realm of things, the meaning of something else, the symbol or system of symbols" (*FF*, 28). Finally, what goes on in the composer's mind seems to be essential to Langer's account of how music symbolizes; she expresses this understanding in a passage in which she also clearly distinguishes her theory from others about the relation of music and the emotions:

> . . . the function of music is not stimulation of feeling, but expression of it; and furthermore, not the symptomatic expression of feelings that beset the composer but a symbolic expression of the forms of sentience as he understands them. It bespeaks his imagination of feelings rather than his own emotional state, and expresses what he *knows about* the so-called "inner life"; and this may exceed his personal case, because music is a symbolic form to him through which he may learn as well as utter ideas of human sensibility. (*FF*, 28)

I return to something that these final few words suggest as, in subsequent chapters, I develop a yet more radical version of the inherent-representational theory of music and the emotions, arguing that neither composers' intentions (or other states of mind) nor listeners' regardings (or other conscious thoughts) are essential to the correct account of how music represents the emotions. In any case, it is now patent that Langer has addressed the matter of the asymmetry of representation as contrasted with the symmetry of isomorphism. We can turn to the third main feature of her theory.

We have already taken notice of the logical independence of the ineffability thesis from the isomorphism and representation theses, nor does Langer say or suggest anything to the contrary. But it does, for Langer, play an important role in her overall account of music insofar as it provides a *reason* why music exists; namely, to reveal certain facts that are of interest to human beings that language proper as well as other symbolisms are incapable of describing or symbolizing. Music, in other words, is a source of *knowledge* about certain features of reality and, at least in some important respects, the *only* source of that knowledge. The sense of 'reason' that is involved here is somewhat obscure insofar as, if the thesis is to be even initially plausible, it cannot refer to the self-acknowledged beliefs and motives of composers many if not most of whom would vehemently deny any such "reasons" for composing. Once again, this is a matter to which I shall return. But just what is Langer's version of the ineffability thesis?

With respect to what music can do that language cannot, Langer states the main idea in these words: "that *music articulates forms which language cannot set forth*"(*PNK*, 233). In this she follows, among many musicians, Wagner, who said (as quoted by Langer) that music expresses ". . . just what is unspeakable in verbal language" (*PNK*, 235). In the context of music, her argument is just that "Because the forms of human feeling are much more congruent with musical forms than with the forms of language, music can *reveal* the nature of feelings with a detail and truth that language cannot approach" (*PNK*, 235).

Although she devotes a substantial amount of space to the topic of ineffability in *Philosophy in a New Key*, Langer has little to say about the precise reason that language is not suited, or not as well suited as music, to describing or "revealing" the emotions. And the reasons she does give seem to admit of either a more radical or a less radical theory about the nature of the ineffable. The more radical version seems to be implied in a passage that follows extensive discussion of positivistic critiques of metaphysics and their consequent relegation to the realm of mere feeling of the "unspeakable" (as Wittgenstein is noted by Langer as calling it). Quoting Bertrand Russell as allowing that "if there be a world which is not physical, or not in space-time, it may have a structure which we can never hope to express or to know . . . ," her words, in partial agreement and partial disagreement, follow:

> Now, I do not believe that "there is a world which is not physical, or not in space-time," but I do believe that in this physical, space-time world of our experience *there are things which do not fit the grammatical*

scheme of expression. But they are not necessarily blind, inconceivable, mystical affairs; they are simply matters which require to be conceived through some symbolistic schema other than discursive language. (*PNK*, 88, my emphasis)

Here Langer seems to be saying, or strongly suggesting, that, to use the language she herself has used approvingly, there are states of affairs or complexes of a certain kind that do not have the same logical form as any propositions of any possible language; there are "ungrammatical" states of affairs in reality itself, and any attempt to express them adequately in any possible language must necessarily fail. Presuming that one could, nevertheless, identify and name the simple constituents of such ungrammatical complexes, the strings of words that would purport to describe any such complex would be, in the semi-technical language of the logician, *ill-formed*, that is, ungrammatical in the way that "Is red tomato the" is ungrammatical.

But the suggestion of a less radical version of the ineffability thesis— one that might still be adequate to her purpose of maintaining that music exists partly because it can express features of reality that language cannot—can be found elsewhere in the same book in these words: "A composer not only indicates, but *articulates* subtle complexes of feeling that language cannot even name, let alone set forth . . ." (*PNK*, 222). This could be read as a restatement of the more radical version of ineffability, but the use of the word *subtle* suggests that it could also be taken only to say that while the forms of these ineffable states of affairs are perfectly "grammatical," language does not possess, nor could it possess at least in practice, the means to capture the minute and infinite nuances of "character" that those states of affairs possess. Put in the language of "subject-predicate," one could say that while the relevant states of affairs are, like all others, of the subject-predicate form, that is, involve the exemplification of certain properties and relations by certain individual things or subjects, the predicates of any possible language are quite inadequate to the richness and subtlety and variety and sheer cardinality of the properties of those individual things and subjects. While some especially good poets can go further than the rest of us in capturing in words the character of the inner life, even they, on this thesis, must necessarily fall short; there is not and cannot be a way to capture in language every subtle difference in the nature of feeling and mood and emotion.

It is by now clear that the more radical version has to do with the *forms* of mental life while the less radical with the *contents*. But which version does Langer actually hold? Even from the texts cited, and adding what little else one can find in her books, I think it must be admitted that the preponderance of the evidence leads us to conclude that she holds the more radical version of the ineffability thesis. Her emphasis on "forms" and the "morphology" of the emotions, as contrasted with their contents, only strengthens this conclusion. But I have introduced this issue at some length partly because I shall later reject the more radical and defend the less radical thesis myself. In doing so, however, I may be committing myself to a more radical thesis as to what it is, exactly, that music represents; namely, the contents and not the forms.

One other feature of Langer's theory must be mentioned in this brief exposition, although the idea of it has been alluded to above: the notion of music as "unconsummated symbol." Part of this idea is that while music does indeed symbolize the emotions, it does not *assert* anything about them. While Langer occasionally refers to truth in art, she does not mean this in the literal sense as it applies to certain mental states and, derivatively, to certain sentences. A piece or passage of music no more has a truth value than a picture has a truth value. The other part of the notion of unconsummated symbol is that the musical symbol is, in Langer's words, "a significant form without conventional significance" (*PNK*, 241)—the fact that, unlike words, musical elements have no "meaning" outside some larger context in which they are placed. Whereas the word *red* has at least some "meaning" independent of any sentence in which it might occur, the note E-flat above middle C has no "meaning" independent of a passage or piece in which it might occur. (There are those who might dispute this to some degree, for example, because of the fact that some people associate certain pitches with certain moods. But it would probably not be disputed that any such associations can be fully overcome by certain contexts in which any given pitch might occur.)

This idea of "significant form without conventional significance," which to some might seem to cast doubt on the entire theory of musical symbolism, Langer sees as an advantage of the theory, in that it accounts for what she calls "the real power of music" in that "it can be 'true' to the life of feeling in a way that language cannot; for its significant forms have that *ambivalence* of content which words cannot have" (*PNK*, 243). And the idea further helps to explain, in Langer's judgment, the different and conflicting attitudes about so-called program music, music that, in some relevant way, is connected with particular persons or events or places. Langer appears to think poorly of program music in general, but is especially harsh in her judgment of those who, as listeners or, even worse, as teachers or composers, would regard a "program" as important or essential to musical value or pleasure. Such an attitude, natural and even common in "musically limited persons" (*PNK*, 243), is, she insists, "really a denial of the true nature of music, which is unconventionalized, unverbalized freedom of thought" (*PNK*, 243), that is, music as unconsummated symbol.

This summary of Susanne Langer's theory of the nature of music as being a symbolism of the realm of the emotions is, while shaped in no small measure by my own theoretical preoccupations, intended all the same to be a reasonably neutral and adequate account of the essentials of that theory. The theory in fact has received little acceptance among philosophers who are cognizant of it, despite occasional half-hearted salutes in its direction, while receiving in some quarters smaller or greater degrees of criticism and rejection. In the Appendix, I summarize the major criticisms in the literature and indicate some measure of reply to those criticisms, especially where they might seem to be applicable to my own version of a representative theory of music.

Susanne Langer set the terms for all subsequent discussion of the idea that music is a symbolism. In my judgment, the theory is, in its essentials, correct. But it contains, all the same, many inadequacies and omissions. Most importantly, it advances no real explanation of *why* sounds should have the importance they obviously do have in human emotional life, that is, why music is so important to human beings. More precisely and more fairly, it fails to present an *ontological* account of the nature of sound and the nature of consciousness to undergird the idea that sounds might represent certain kinds of conscious states to human beings. The next three chapters are intended to provide that ontological account along with a treatment of representation that is, for better or worse, rather different from any in the literature.

3

Representation

There is reason in choosing as one's most general notion in the domain of reference, symbolism, aboutness, intentionality, and ofness that of *representation*. Still, the word has its disadvantages, especially in its suggestion that whatever is doing the representing somehow only "again" or "indirectly" brings before the mind something that could be simply presented. This is a disadvantage for two reasons, one general and the other particular to the context of discussion of Langer's theory.

The general reason is that in the fundamental form of representation, which is that of consciousness itself, there is of necessity no distinction between presentation and representation except in an altogether different sense. Indeed, to regard consciousness itself as a form of representation (which I shall do for reasons I hope to make clear) invites unfortunate associations with theories of perception known as representationalism (or representism or representative realism), which are rightly discredited for positing some kind of intermediary, whether called an "idea" or a "sense" or "sense data," between the act of awareness and its object. The particular reason derives from the fact, as the reader may recall, that Langer herself characterizes symbols in the arts as "presentational," contrasting them, to be sure, not with "representational" but with "discursive" symbols.

The main advantage to the language of representation is its indifference to the notion of truth. Paintings represent people and ruins and bowls of fruit without thereby being either true or false. Representation as such is not assertion or affirmation, although—and this may be the best way to think about the mainly linguistic contexts in which truth and falsity are involved—one can assert that a certain representation is or is not faithful to its object or that its object does or does not exist. The other relevant advantage is that, in anthropological fact, the language of representation is the broadest and most common.

There is no possibility of characterizing or even listing all the specific contexts to which the language of representation reasonably can be applied; but it will be valuable to mention at least the three major realms in which, to varying degrees, representation is involved in a defining or essential way. Those realms are *consciousness, language,* and *art.* And there are two other major domains of human experience in which representation (or what in these cases is more likely to be called symbolism) is thought to be very important although not, perhaps, in the same essential manner. Those realms are *dreams* and *religion,* understanding religion in a broad sense as including both ritual and myth. We may proceed by categorizing these five domains or, more precisely, their elements by the *kinds* of entities that are, or are said to be, the sort of thing that does the representing. These kinds, not quite exclusive of one another nor strictly matching one-to-one to the five domains, are also five in number: *awarenesses, words and sentences, art objects, dreams,* and *behaviors.* Dreams are a species of awarenesses and religion involves at least awarenesses, words and sentences, and behaviors.

Awarenesses are to be understood as including all forms of consciousness, including perceptions and dreams as well as imaginings, desirings, rememberings, contemplatings, feelings (in many senses, including the having of moods, emotions, and bodily sensations), introspections, and more—in short, everything whatsoever that is part of the stream of consciousness. Nor, of course, are awarenesses limited to humans; we know that other terrestrial beings, probably including very simple organisms, have perceptions and pains and, as in the case of the sonar capability of bats, other forms of awareness that we cannot fully imagine. And we must not exclude the possibility that elsewhere than Earth there are conscious forms of life and possibly conscious artifacts all with their own forms of awareness. Finally, we must also acknowledge that there are awarenesses of which we are not aware. That is, we are aware of certain things without knowing that we are aware of them. Thus awareness includes *conscious awareness* and *unconscious awareness,* as I shall call them, both however being part of what we loosely call "the stream of consciousness."

It would be foolish to try to say exactly what a *word* or a *sentence* is; I will observe only that each is, or contains, an artifact of a very special kind, the difference between written and spoken language involving that artifactual component. (Sign language is variously deemed a *language* or a *behavior*, though with no doubt about its status as a form of representation.) *Art objects* are to be understood to include not only those semi-permanent physical objects that first come to mind, such as paintings, sculptures, and buildings, but also performances such as dances, recitals, and actings in plays. Indeed, for our purposes, there need be no limit on the kind of entity that is regarded as an art object, and no theory will be advanced in these pages as to what, if anything, delimits the realm of art objects beyond human choice. As to what entities count as *behaviors* and *dreams*, it is reasonably self-evident just what kinds of things in the world, including our minds, we are talking about.

A representation is anything whatsoever that serves to *bring to mind*, in either conscious or unconscious awareness, something (whether existent or not) other than itself. I say this not in the spirit of insightful (or shallow) "conceptual analysis" nor as mere stipulation but as presumed fact of linguistic anthropology. If it is not such fact, then do take it as stipulation; in any case the notion of bringing to mind is fundamental to understanding language, artworks, and awareness itself. And much of distinctly human awareness is the product of our representations, especially of words and similar artifacts.

Two further points may be touched on in these preliminary remarks on the notion of bringing to mind. As I shall write, certain constituents of awarenesses are representations. That is, awareness itself brings things to mind. To be sure, in that case the representation and its effect—bringing to mind—amount to virtually the same entity or event, but I hope to persuade the reader in succeeding paragraphs and the next chapter that this is, all the same, a useful categorization. The other point requires elaboration of the fact that a person can be aware of something, have something brought to mind, without knowing then or at any other time that he or she is so aware. There is much of which we are aware, as shown in our behavior, that is not part of our conscious experience or our "attending" awareness, some of which awareness we may even sincerely deny having. This is, of course, part of the notion of the unconscious; and, as I have already indicated, it will play a fundamental role in the chapters that follow.

I propose to distinguish three kinds of representation: *conventional* representation; *natural* representation; and what, for want of a better expression, I shall call *quasi-natural* representation. Although I shall discuss each separately later in this chapter, a preliminary characterization may be helpful. A *conventional representation* is one in which there is nothing in the nature of the representation and nothing in the nature of its user that indicates or specifies or determines that it shall represent what it does represent. By the greatest possible contrast, a *natural representation* is one in which the representation, by its inherent nature, determines both *that* and *what* it represents. Finally, "between" conventional and natural representation, a *quasi-natural* representation is one that, with respect to some species, is such that, given both the nature of the representation and the nature of that species, it does in *lawful* necessity represent what it does represent to the members of that species. Defining these notions in this or any other way does not, of course, imply that anything actually satisfies any of the definitions; and it is surely the case that many, perhaps most, philosophers would deny that there is any such thing as either natural or quasi-natural representation. Theories of natural representation have been widely criticized in the literature or else simply assumed to be false or incoherent. For one typical example, Hilary Putnam criticizes such theories as being "magical theories of reference."[1] As for the idea of quasi-natural representation, one simply doesn't find it discussed as such in the literature even though Freud's theory of symbolism in dreams may reasonably be understood as involving such a notion. But it may be assumed that any claim of quasi-natural representations is likely to receive much the same hostility as do theories of natural representation.

With respect to these notions, I maintain the following theses: (1) the most important form of conventional representation is that of *language*; (2) the only form of natural representation is that of *awareness*; and (3) the most interesting form of quasi-natural representation, with the possible exception of dreams, is that of *music*. I hold further that conventional representation and quasi-natural representation both presuppose, although in different ways, the phenomenon of natural representation, that is, awareness itself. Put another way: if there were no awareness, there would be and could be nothing at all that would be a representation of any kind. Awareness is the fundamental form of representation and the basis, in various ways, of all other forms of representation. None

---

[1] Hilary Putnam, *Reason, Truth, and History* (Cambridge: Cambridge University Press, 1981), 3.

of what we call maps, pictures, blueprints, words, or anything else would be *of* or *about* anything were awareness not to exist. Put a little more technically, there is no two-term relation of *aboutness* in the world independent of awareness, whatever relations of *resemblance* and *causation* there are in nature itself. The nature of awareness is the subject of the next chapter. We need now to look more closely at resemblance.

We have long since learned that what a given person or population of persons takes as *similar* or *alike* depends on many factors, including those of kinds called environmental and cultural. Numerous psychological experiments, anthropological investigations, and linguistic studies attest to the relative plasticity of the human mind in this regard, and we know the power of our biological needs at one point and that of the arts at another to move us, sometimes even force us, to make distinctions or to conceive similarities where others do not or we did not before. Still, few would say that there are no resemblances in nature itself, no similarities that are objective in the sense of being independent of human linguistic and cultural choices and practices. What makes two hydrogen atoms both atoms of the hydrogen kind is surely, on all accounts (whatever some postmodernists and other relativists may imagine themselves to believe), due to inherent resemblance between those atoms, based on possession of the same properties. In short, resemblance *is* in nature itself in the precise sense that it would be there even if consciousness did not exist, just as it was there for the billions of years before consciousness did exist.

The objective nature of resemblance, combined with the fact that representation presupposes the existence of consciousness, entails that in no case is resemblance a sufficient condition for representation. The long temptation, at least in Western thought on the subject, has been to suppose that if resemblance were not a sufficient condition for representation (did anyone ever *really* believe that it was?), then it was at least a necessary one or at least a condition that was in fact involved in all cases of representation that were not purely conventional; the irrelevance of whatever similarity there is—and there is necessarily some —between the word *red* and the color red to the representation of the latter by the former has long been recognized. From theories of perception to theories of the arts above all, only over the last several decades has resemblance come to lose its appeal as the heart of the matter of representation.

Broadly speaking, once one abandons resemblance as the heart of the matter in representation, one goes in one of three directions: (1) one may come to say that what was previously thought to be a case of representation due to some natural or inherent connection between the putative representing object and the putative represented one was, after all, just another case of conventional representation, that is, a matter of *choice*; or (2) one may argue that, as a special case of the first and in keeping with the fashions of the day in analytic philosophy, it is not just a straight matter of choice: what matters is the existence of another kind of natural relation, the *causal* one, between what is represented and the object that represents it; or (3) one may maintain that there is an inherent relation of representation itself or, as it is more likely to be called, of *intentionality*, of a *sui generis* sort; that is, of a sort that is not to be analyzed or otherwise understood exhaustively by way of relations and properties that did or could exist in a world without consciousness.

None of this is to deny, however, that in fact resemblance often does play a significant role in some forms of representation; and there will be a residue of that idea ultimately even in my own account of how music, through intentionality, represents possible states of consciousness. But especially since Nelson Goodman's *Languages of Art*, we have begun to grasp how difficult it is to specify exactly what the resemblance is between, say, a certain painting and a certain portion of the Earth's surface, and just what role that resemblance, assuming it to be relevantly there at all, plays in making the picture *of* that landscape, that is, a representation of it.[2] When a child insists that the drawing she has just completed is a picture of a cow in response to the suggestion of an adult that it is a nice picture of a boat, we may well wonder if there is any single answer to the question of what the drawing *really* represents. Reflection may also suggest that while the adult presumed to rely on some perceived resemblance of the drawing to a boat—or at least its greater resemblance to a boat than any other object from among the vague class of "possible" objects—the child was, unknowingly, relying on *creator's intentions*, a form of conventionalism to whatever extent we are prepared to say that the result does represent a cow. Perhaps just making these and further distinctions—while abandoning any attempt to say that a painting, in any case, must "really" represent just one and only

[2]   Nelson Goodman, *Languages of Art: An Approach to a Theory of Symbols* (Indianapolis: Hackett, 1976); *LA* in the text.

one kind, or member of a kind, of object—solves some of these puzzles. To take another kind of example that I have used in a different connection: assuming that mental images are entities that can resemble physical objects, when I see my friend, whom I was imagining shortly before, and find, after twenty years of separation, that my image more closely resembles his accompanying son than it does or ever did resemble him, shall we say that my imagin*ing* was not, as I supposed, of the father after all? I would think the answer is surely negative—for whatever that shows about the place of images in imagining. But it remains the case that the role resemblance plays in many different modes of representation itself varies along many dimensions.

It is widely supposed that resemblance is a crucial feature of representation just to the extent that representation is natural and not conventional; and descriptions and theories abound that embody this supposition. Yet, if I am not mistaken, something very nearly the opposite of this is the truth of the matter. Closer examinations of the notions of conventional representation, quasi-natural representation, and natural representation will make this heresy seem more plausible.

Conventional representation, of which everyday language seems to be the clearest and most important instance, I characterized as a form of representation that depends on neither the inherent nature of the representation nor that of the one who uses that representation. This is not to say that there is no cause or explanation of why, say, for a certain class of humans, the inscription *red* represents the color red. Such a denial would be absurd. It is, however, to say that the explanation, in its essential part, lies neither in examining or understanding more intimately the word *red* itself (whether as type or as token, and whether or not as combined with certain human thoughts, dispositions, and intentions) nor in knowing or invoking human nature. That there is an explanation of some kind is presupposed by that form of conventionalism that is the "causal" theory of representation, this theory being, once more, not the truism that there is a causal explanation of any particular case of representation but the insistence that the causal connection between the representing object and the represented object is, analytically speaking, what makes it the case that the one represents the other.

The key feature of conventional representation, as I believe it is most usefully characterized, is that of *choice*, although this "choice" will not typically appear to be that at all, embodied as it will be in tradition and culture. Whether in language or in painting, what makes the features of the representing object "in fact" represent what they do represent is something that in principle could be changed by choice, difficult as that might be, even as communities sometimes deliberately alter their languages (as, for example, the Dutch did in combining the formerly gendered articles *den* and *de* into the common *de* early in the twentieth century). Again, one need not deny that certain "objective" resemblances may be playing some role in the representation in emphasizing that which ones of them are doing so and to what extent is itself a matter of choice, tradition, culture, and style. And one need not share the idealistic taint in Goodman's claim that "Resemblance and deceptiveness, far from being constant and independent sources and criteria of representational practice are in some degree products of it" (*LA*, 39) in order to agree with him that realism in painting, often thought to be the clearest case of representation by resemblance, is not in fact a matter of resemblance pure and simple (a painting of a landscape arguably resembles another painting more than it resembles any landscape) but instead of the ease with which the observer, familiar with the style, can be informed of the relevant features of what is represented. And this is a matter of applying rules of correlation, which rules are determined not by nature but by choice and culture.

Conventional representation, we may now say schematically, is a *three-term* relation among the representing object, the represented object, and the representer, the last being the one who creates or observes or otherwise is relevantly affected by the representation as a representation. This feature of being a three-term relation is also a defining one of quasi-natural representation.

In my account, natural representation, yet to be discussed in any detail, is the fundamental form of representation. Yet quasi-natural representation is the most complex and, especially if it exists, in many respects the most interesting form of representation. Considering only the human case, we may say that there is quasi-natural representation if, *due to the nature of some kind of object and due to human nature*, an instance of that kind of object does, when appropriately presented to a human being, actually represent some particular object (kind or particular) to that person. This, then, is a kind of representation that is beyond human choice although, as always, whatever does represent in this way, if anything, may also represent in the conventional way to the extent that anything whatsoever can be stipulated to represent anything whatsoever.

It might be argued that both human nature and the natures of representing objects are always involved in representation at least to the extent that the representing object, if it is to be such in any systematic way, must be of a sort that is easily perceivable by human beings, something that human beings can manipulate and rearrange, and so on. I have no objection to the idea that there is a continuum and not a clear delineation between conventional representation and quasi-natural representation; it is surely the case that, due to human nature, there are limits on the forms that a natural language can or will take, to mention the most important case, where "forms" refers to syntax as much as inscription and phoneme. And it probably will not be doubted that the fact that humans have such extensive conventional systems of representation at all is due to, and importantly expressive of, our human nature. But even if it is the case that the forms of all representation depend, in some way, on the nature of the human mind, the distinction between conventional representation and quasi-natural representation is not thereby unserviceable. For the ways and degrees of such involvement vary widely, and it is well to have the distinction as made before us even if the lines between and among the forms are not precise.

Quasi-natural representation, we noted earlier, is, like conventional representation, a *three-term* relation involved the representing object, that which is represented, and the representer (here, more interestingly, the person *to* whom something is represented as contrasted with the creator, if any, of the representing object even if, as in the case of dreams, this is one and the same person). Whatever isomorphism or resemblance may exist between the entities that are the representing objects and the "entities" ("they" may not exist, of course) that are represented, there is no simple or natural relation of representation between them. The one represents the other only *to* or *for* a person in some way *because* of the nature of the human mind—the mind as *intermediary* in a broad but proper use of that word—but here in respect of its nature and not of its will or choice. As long as we are talking about representation as a three-term relation, be it conventional or quasi-natural or something in between, we have not come across the purest form of representation— that in which, due to its nature alone, the representing object manages to represent something else. To this notion I now turn.

Something is a natural representation of something else if it is such that, by its very nature, it does represent that something else, that is, if it is an *intrinsically intentional* entity. In an earlier book, on the subject of intentionality, I used the expression 'natural sign' for this notion, follow-ing the 'signum naturale' of the fourteenth-century philosopher, Wil-liam of Occam.[3] Although the expression 'natural sign' has continued to be used in this sense sporadically during the intervening centuries, there is another, far more common use in which, for example, smoke is a natural sign of fire. In this use, the expression refers to mere causal connection and does not involve anything like representation in the sense of symbolizing or pointing to. So, although I gave my earlier book its title from that expression, here I shall, for the most part, continue to write of natural *representation*.

Stipulating that there is natural representation only when the repre-sentation is intrinsically intentional will probably suggest that such representation is by definition such that only awareness itself can be or involve such representation. I believe the suggestion to be correct, but I do not wish to argue the definitional point. The only case I know of in which it has been maintained that there are intrinsically intentional entities that are not states of mind or constituents thereof is Gottlob Frege's theory of senses. Senses are supposed to be entities that are neither mental nor physical but inhabitants of a "third realm." These senses, argued by Frege to be necessary to account for certain facts about consciousness without falling into the errors of psychologism, are said to be eternal, mind-independent entities that are by their nature intentional and such that each, by its nature, represents a particular state of affairs. In *Natural Signs* I argued that the facts that Frege wishes to explain by senses can better be accounted for by the theory of natural signs and without subjecting oneself to the fallacies of psychologism. So, while granting the possibility that it is Frege who is right and I wrong, I nonetheless proceed on the assumption that if there is natural representation at all, it exists only in states of awareness, though not by any means limited to the human mind.

Consciousness, Husserl and Sartre were wont to say, is always con-sciousness *of* something, although not necessarily of "something" that exists. This is so much the case that when one tries to specify the char-acter of any particular state of consciousness—be it a perception or a re-membering or a desiring or a contemplating or an imagining or what-ever—one can, apart from mention of its "formal" characteristics as an

---

[3]   Laird Addis, *Natural Signs: A Theory of Intentionality* (Philadelphia: Temple University Press, 1989), 37.

event (such as those of duration and intensity), only describe what that consciousness was *about*. To describe one's perceptions of a parade is to describe the parade—as perceived, to be sure, but even so the parade is not any perception of it. Thus, to put the point paradoxically, to describe a state of consciousness is to describe something other than the state of consciousness, that which the consciousness is a consciousness *of*.[4]

This paradoxical feature of consciousness is part of what Sartre was relying on in characterizing consciousness as a "nothingness." Another part of what he meant, seeming to believe that the former implied the latter, is that there is nothing in a state of consciousness itself that indicates in any way what that consciousness is a consciousness of, just as there is nothing in the desk on which I now write that indicates in any way that it stands in a certain spatial relation to the Eiffel Tower. In this denial of intrinsically intentional entities, Sartre is, in my judgment, profoundly in error, as I argue in the next chapter. But I could not agree with him more in his initial claim that consciousness never lacks an object and that in a certain sense its *ofness* is what makes it a state of consciousness.

Consciousness (or, more broadly, awareness) is the one and only form of natural representation.[5] That is, a state of consciousness is or contains an entity that by its nature represents what that consciousness is a consciousness of. Thus natural representation is a *two-term* relation and, in an obvious sense, the purest form of representation imaginable, whether or not it actually exists. It doesn't require a third to make the one represent the other either by way of creating the representation or of being represented to: the entity that is the natural representation does, by its nature alone, point to or represent what it does represent.

There is another way to express the distinction between the three-term forms of representation in conventional and quasi-natural representation on the one hand and the two-term from of representation in natural representation on the other. A representing object in either

---

[4]   Such description is only ordinary description as contrasted with ontological description. In the next chapter, I put forth a theory of consciousness that includes ontological description of states of awareness, and these descriptions are about such states themselves and not what they are awarenesses of.

[5]   Because I have already distinguished conscious awareness from unconscious awareness, it is somewhat incongruent terminologically to write of states of consciousness when they include unconscious awarenesses. But it is also often highly convenient; and when there is no possibility of confusion, as in the rest of this paragraph and much of the next chapter, I sometimes do so.

conventional or quasi-natural representation has properties and characters independent of the fact that it is such a representing object: an inscription, a dream, a passage of music, a picture, and anything else said to be a symbol or a representation, except for a natural sign itself, is such that one can examine and describe it without attending to or even knowing the fact that it is a representing object. But a natural sign, an intrinsically intentional entity, essentially exhausts itself in being a representation. (That is the real explanation of Sartre's paradox, and not his denial of the very existence of such entities.) If anything is a naturally representing object, it will not be some ordinary object that has long been known but has not been previously suspected of being a representation. Even those who are skeptical that consciousness is or involves natural representation as I have characterized it must grant that consciousness is the best and probably the only candidate for such status.

But it is now appropriate to turn to the nature of consciousness itself, with the aim of identifying, in the chapter after next, a certain fundamental feature that is possessed only by music and consciousness, and that partly explains how it is that music represents certain possible states of consciousness.

4

Consciousness

Whenever one is conscious, that is, not unconscious or dead, one has a state of consciousness or, more often, a sizable number of states of consciousness. As I write these words, I am attending most strongly to the ideas I am attempting to express. But I am simultaneously aware perceptually of the page on which I write and the pen I use as well as, although with less focus and attention, all the other things in my visual field—the lamp, books, papers, my hands and sweater, and so on. Moreover, at some level of awareness, I am conscious of various bodily sensations—my contact with the chair, my faint hunger, my location in space, and so on. And, too, there hover vague thoughts of what I shall do later today, of my family, and so on. At almost every moment of a person's life, the conscious mind is some kind of complex of many states of consciousness, including perceivings, rememberings, feelings (in both the bodily sense and in that of mood and emotion), desirings, thinkings and contemplatings, imaginings, and so on. Even when one is asleep, one not only dreams (which is best regarded as a form of perceiving, for the most part) but is also rudimentarily aware of one's physical environment and one's internal states of body and mood, especially if they are unusually strong.

Although, in an obvious sense, it is not possible to enumerate and from each other to distinguish each of the awarenesses that constitute a person's conscious mind at a moment, for analytic purposes it is best to regard each as a distinct state of consciousness. At the same time, it is

well to keep in mind the wide range of differences in the levels of awareness that they jointly exemplify and the fact that some, probably only
one at most, of those states of consciousness may have another one of
them as its object. And we may say, trivially but usefully, that for a person to be alive and not unconscious at a moment is just for that person
to have at least one state of consciousness at the time. The same applies
to animals and any other sentient forms of life there are as well as any
artifacts (none here on Earth—yet!) that are conscious. Unless they are
organic, artifacts are not and cannot be *alive* in the sense that applies to
organisms. But whether or not there could be a conscious artifact, that
is, an object with physical states both complex enough and of a nature
to produce consciousness is a purely causal question; whether or not we
humans could ever *know* an artifact to be conscious raises a number of
philosophical questions. (I dismiss as empirically absurd the possibility
of so-called disembodied consciousness, whether in this world or some
fancied other one.)

Some philosophers tell us that consciousness does not exist at all
(eliminative materialism), while some other philosophers insist that
conscious states are just states of the brain as they might be observed by
a neurologist (central-state materialism). And yet other philosophers
maintain that a conscious state is just a disposition to behaviors of a certain kind (ontological behaviorism) or whatever causes behaviors of a
certain kind (ontological functionalism). The inability or unwillingness
of all these philosophers to recognize consciousness as a distinct and
analytically irreducible phenomenon is based mostly on their false supposition that to do so is somehow to be "unscientific" and to reveal oneself as still bound by the superstitions of religion or other prescientific
worldviews.

I have argued elsewhere that a certain kind of dualism, but not a substance dualism, of mind and body is fully compatible with science in
every respect—with its presuppositions, its methods, and its findings
—and that it is not mere adherence to the scientific worldview, which I
completely share, but *scientism* of an occasionally subtle but more often
crude and ontologically naive sort that leads many philosophers to their
various forms of materialism.[1] Being scientifically minded means, at the
least, to be empirically minded. An uninhibited empiricism that takes

---

[1]   Addis, *Natural Signs*, especially the chapter called "Mental Acts and the Scientific
Worldview."

the world, as far as possible, as one finds it while remaining consistent with the findings of science compels anyone whose thought has not been tainted by scientism to recognize that consciousness does exist and that it has features that are neither part of nor reducible to those recognized by any physical science, whether that science be physics itself or behaviorist psychology or neurobiology or anything else.[2]

The absurdity of the various forms of ontological materialism—eliminative, central-state, behaviorist, functionalist—is for me obvious just because some states of consciousness are *given* to me and as having features that show them to be distinct from anything given to the outer senses. While this is not a book in defense of dualism as against materialism, it may be said that should some plausibility be found independently in the theory of the relation of mind to music to be developed in subsequent chapters, that theory can only support the theory of the nature of consciousness that underlies it. That theory is one within a framework of property dualism, according to which there are distinct realms of mental properties and physical properties, neither realm being ontologically reducible to the other.

As I have also argued in *Natural Signs*, the choice between dualism and materialism is something that is not ultimately amenable to argument.[3] One's choice, instead, reflects whether that philosopher regards the *given* (as determined by enlightened everyday experience) or the *basic* (as determined by fundamental physical science) as the starting place of philosophy. Either starting place is perfectly compatible with basic physics and indeed all of physical science, but I have already suggested that it is not the dualist but instead the materialist who, on what may fairly be called ideological grounds, abandons the scientific worldview when it comes to consciousness. Just as the fundamentalist Christian is prepared to "accept science" up to, but not beyond, the point at which it comes into conflict with the Biblical account of the beginning of the world, so the materialist is prepared to "be empirical" only until that empiricism suggests that the realm of the physical is not all there is

---

[2]   Here by 'reducible' I mean the idea that a mental feature is the same thing as some physical thing. Reducibility by laws is another matter, for it preserves the *ontological non-identity* of what is reduced to that to which it is reduced. There is no good reason to doubt the complete reducibility of mind to matter in this sense. Another way to say this is that it is lawfully impossible for two physically identical beings to have qualitatively different minds. But the primacy of matter to mind is not the same thing as the identity of mind to (some states of) matter.

[3]   See the chapter called "Consciousness and the Starting Place of Philosophy."

in this world, indeed not all there is "in" each of us or any conscious being. But, again, we may agree and even insist on the profound causal intimacy of consciousness and the brain (in us) and fully accept that when the brain dies, the consciousness that was dependent on it ceases forever.

Consider again my perception of the paper on the desk before me. Like every state of consciousness this perception is an event in time with certain distinguishing features or properties. For one, it is a state of consciousness and not a chair or a star or a political revolution. Furthermore, it is a state of consciousness that is a perceiving and not an imagining or a remembering or a doubting or a desiring or any other mode of awareness. Finally, it is a perceiving of a particular piece of paper and not of a cow or a person or any other piece of paper. So we may say, in a preliminary schema, that the three crucial features of this perceiving as a state of consciousness are just that it is a state of *consciousness*, that it is a *perceiving*, and that it is *of this piece of paper*. Ontological understanding of these features (I ignore the feature of its being *my* perceiving) is virtually identical to understanding what a mind is. And if one also holds, as is plausible, that to be a state of consciousness just is to be a perceiving or an imagining or some other mode of awareness and also to be *of* something or other, then we may attend only to the two features of (1) being a *perceiving* and (2) being *of* this piece of paper. To have ontological understanding of consciousness is then, or so I am suggesting, to have such understanding of what grounds the *mode* of an awareness (in this case, of its being a perceiving) and of what grounds its *intentionality* (in this case, of its being of a certain piece of paper).

So let us proceed by considering the feature of being a perceiving. What makes a state of consciousness a perceiving instead of, say, an imagining? In the philosophical tradition, one finds four basic answers to the question among those who take the issue seriously, that is, among those who do not deny the existence or distinctive nature of consciousness. Those answers, and some of their primary proponents, are (1) that what makes this a perceiving is a peculiar quality or "vivacity" of the *sense materials* involved in perception (David Hume); or (2) that what makes this a perceiving is just that it is an awareness of a "perceived object" (Jean-Paul Sartre); or (3) that what makes this a perceiving is that there is a *relation* of perceiving between the perceiver and the object perceived (G. E. Moore and Bertrand Russell); or (4) that what makes this a perceiving is that the state of consciousness has the *monadic property* of being-a-perceiving (Gustav Bergmann and Edmund Husserl).

The first two answers maintain that it is a feature of the *objects* of awareness and not of the awareness itself that makes the awareness the mode of consciousness that it is, and seems thereby committed to the conclusion that one cannot perceive exactly the same object that earlier one only imagined or later remembered. The third answer raises the problem of how a descriptive relation (as contrasted with a logical relation) can hold between something that exists—the perceiver—and "something" that does not exist, as when someone perceives (or, as we would say, hallucinates) a pink elephant. For a variety of reasons, some more of which I come to later, it seems that only the fourth answer is entirely adequate and most faithfully reflects ontologically the commonsense linguistic and phenomenological facts that it is *my* state of consciousness that is a perceiving, that is, that it is some feature of *me* and not of something other than me as the first two views explicitly hold and, to a lesser degree, the third view would also have it. In Hume's case, the motive was to have an actless ontology of mind, something which he mistakenly believed was required by his nonsubstantialism; in Sartre's case the motivation is also affected by his anti-substantialism of mind but in the sense that, he believes, to suppose that there is anything "in" the mind itself would suggest that the mind is a substance or at least a "thing" and so deny us our "freedom." The third view, which grounds the mode of awareness in a relation between the perceiver and the perceived object, is a view strongly suggested by language ("I perceive a piece of paper"), and for Moore and others got its plausibility partly just because they were impressed by the forms of grammar and partly too, I suggest, because they simply didn't conceive or consider any alternatives. One looks in vain for any real formulation of, much less argument against, the alternatives to this view in the literature in which it is advocated.[4]

But let us look now at the other feature of the state of consciousness— that it is *of* a certain piece of paper; for the best arguments in favor of what I believe is the correct view on this matter are also the best ones, with the exception of one that is irrelevant, for the correct view as to

[4] I am thinking especially of G. E. Moore, "The Subject Matter of Psychology," *Proceedings of the Aristotelian Society* 10 (1910); and Bertrand Russell, "Knowledge by Acquaintance and Knowledge by Description," in his *Mysticism and Logic and Other Essays* (Totowa, N.J.: Barnes and Noble, 1981).

what grounds the mode feature. The common thread is in the idea that both features are grounded in *monadic* properties of the state of consciousness itself and not anything "outside" or other than it.

It is not as easy to list the distinct answers in the tradition to the question of what makes a state of consciousness *of* or *about* just what it is of or about as it is to list those addressing what makes it the mode of awareness it is. Still we may enumerate at least the following (again with primary proponents): (1) that the perceiving is of just the object it is of because it is *caused* in an appropriate way by that object (Hilary Putnam); or (2) that the perceiving is of just the object it is of because the awareness *just does go* to that particular object much as this desk just does stand in a certain spatial relation to the Eiffel Tower without any further relevant feature of either the desk or the tower (Russell and Sartre); or (3) that the perceiving is of just the object it is of because there is "in" the mind, or "between" the mind and the object of awareness, something that *resembles* that object or is otherwise especially connected to it by some mind- independent relation and of which something the perceiver is aware (Descartes); or (4) that the perceiving is of just the object it is of because the state of consciousness has a property that has come to be *correlated* through the use of language to that object (Wilfrid Sellars and Wittgenstein); or (5) that the perceiving is of just the object it is of because the state of consciousness has a property that is *intrinsically intentional*, that by its inherent nature "points to" the object of awareness (Bergmann and Husserl). Some medieval theories and possibly some later theories may be regarded as combining various of these ideas. For example, the Thomistic abstraction theory of perception would seem to have it that the mind takes on the *form* (whatever that is) of the object perceived, as the third answer might have it, thus giving the perceiver the *kind* of the object of perception while that object causes certain "phantasms" in the senses of the perceiver, as the first answer might have it, thus accounting for its being a perceiving of this particular instance of the kind.

In the third chapter of *Natural Signs*, I gave three detailed arguments for supposing that the last of these answers—that which countenances simple, monadic properties of states of consciousness that are intrinsically intentional—to be the correct solution. Here I shall only summarize these arguments, which I continue to find compelling. Of the three arguments, the first and second also argue in favor of a view that what accounts for the other feature—its being a perceiving and not some other mode of awareness—is also due to a simple monadic property of the state of consciousness. The three arguments I have labeled as the *scientific* argument, the *phenomenological* argument, and the *dialectical* argument.

The scientific argument maintains that what makes my perceiving a perceiving *of* that piece of paper (and not of a cow or anything else) must be a property of me (and not a property of the object I perceive or any relation between me and it or the mere fact that my perceiving was caused in a certain way) because, in causal fact, a person's behavior varies systematically according to what it is that one is perceiving. Exactly the same point applies to its being a perceiving and not an imagining or any other mode of awareness. Thus there must be something about the *person* and not just the objects of awareness and the relations between the person and those objects that explains this systematic variation; that is, some (monadic) *properties* of that person. It is particularly clear that the explanation of such variations in behavior cannot be due to the objects themselves or any relation to them in the cases in which those "objects" do not exist: thinking of unicorns has different causal consequences from thinking of mermaids if only in the linguistic dispositions that are acquired, but those differences cannot be accounted for by differences between unicorns and mermaids for there are none of either kind. Yet thinking of a unicorn is different from thinking of a mermaid. The difference must be "in" the thinker.

So far this argument shows only that what makes a state of consciousness of what it is of (and the mode it is) must be properties of the *person* whose behavior is only thereby explained. But if one wishes to say further, as one should, that our behavior is determined in part by the nature of our mental life, then one is entitled to conclude more specifically that these must be properties of our states of consciousness themselves. Thus we may conclude from the scientific argument that every state of consciousness has a property that specifies what that state of consciousness is a consciousness of, and another property that specifies what mode of awareness it is. Otherwise, there is no way to explain how it is that our behavior varies systematically with both of these features of consciousness.

The *phenomenological* argument to the conclusion that every state of consciousness exemplifies instances of each of the two kinds of properties is *not*, as might initially be supposed, merely the insistence that introspection reveals a property of each kind in the case of any state of consciousness that one happens to introspect to the conclusion that those properties are there, as theorized. I do believe that we can and do find those properties by introspection; but arguments from introspection are rarely convincing to those not already persuaded. My argument is different, and relies on certain data that any theory of the nature of consciousness must accommodate.

It is a datum that when I am imagining, say, that Sirius has ten planets I can know, if I care to reflect on the matter, that I am imagining and not, say, remembering or perceiving or doubting or anything else. It is also a datum that I can know, in similar fashion, that it is *of* Sirius's having ten planets I am imagining and not, say, of my swimming the Atlantic Ocean or of talking with Socrates or anything else. I submit that the best explanation, and probably the only plausible explanation, of these data is that I am, or can become, directly acquainted with whatever it is in the world that permits me such knowledge. For I know these facts with the same immediacy and certainty that one knows one has a headache and without, therefore, the degree of doubt that attaches to any belief one has about things uncontroversially (except among a few philosophers) external to oneself. And I do mean here not rational certainty—it's not really a question of being justified—but of psychological certainty, the felt conviction one has or may have about both the mode of awareness one has and what that awareness is of, combined with the conviction that no possible counterevidence could change those convictions at the moment. High degrees of psychological certainty may attach also to beliefs about matters external to oneself but, with many qualifications that we cannot make our business here, everyone allows the possibility of falsification about such matters—if not in words, then in deeds, as in the case of religious believers who, while denying in words the possibility that their beliefs are false, show their insecurities in their emphasis on faith and their defensiveness in challenges to their beliefs. In any case, we are looking here for the *best* explanation of the data.

We already know what some of the alternative views are as to the "location" of what it is that grounds the two features in question; they would put the ground either in the object of awareness itself or in some connection to the object (or one in each, as Moore and Russell appear to have held). These views, I further submit, make those grounds too "distant" from the person whose state of consciousness it is adequately to explain the two data. Each view is analogous to supposing that I could tell that I stand in a certain spatial relation to the Eiffel Tower just by standing in that relation. But I cannot tell—either that I stand in a spatial relation to it at all or that it is of just such and such a distance in a certain direction. Nor will introspection help because there is nothing relevant to introspect. Modeling consciousness on descriptive relations such as, for example, spatial relations is a mistake in almost every regard. Because I can tell immediately that I am imagining and that it is of Sirius's having ten planets, we are forced to conclude that what grounds these features must be "in" the state of consciousness itself by way of being monadic properties of it.

Anyone who has found my argument plausible so far probably will agree without further argument that the property that makes my state of consciousness an imagining may reasonably be called the property of *being-an-imagining* which it is, so to speak, in and of itself. But some who agree that there is a property of any state of consciousness that grounds what that state of consciousness is of will deny that *being-of-Sirius's-having-ten-planets* is just that property, in and of itself. Instead, they will say that this is the property that, whatever its intrinsic nature, one has learned to *correlate* with a certain object of awareness, in this case Sirius's having ten planets, just as the *words* 'Sirius's having ten planets' have come to be, for certain humans, so correlated. In short, according to this view, mental signs, which on some of these views just are images of words, are, like words themselves, only *conventional* and not *natural* signs. Something of this kind of view, perhaps in an even more radical form, appears to be that of Wittgenstein in his later period, as suggested by his aphorism that "It [a sensation of pain] is not a *something*, but not a *nothing* either" and in his related arguments against the possibility of a so-called private language.[5]

Be that as it may, I submit that the view that we *learn* which mental property picks out which object of awareness is incoherent. For it altogether presupposes exactly what was to be explained: if I am to come to correlate or be informed of an already existing correlation of a certain mental property (or word) to a certain object of awareness, I must already be aware of each separately in order to make or to understand the correlation. And those awarenesses cannot themselves be explained on

[5]   Ludwig Wittgenstein, *Philosophical Investigations*, trans. G. E. M. Anscombe (Oxford: Basil Blackwell, 1953), 102e. In this entry, 304, Wittgenstein's explicit topic is pain and not mental phenomena generally. But he seems to want to apply the idea generally as the next entry, 305, on remembering strongly indicates.

the basis of a learned correlation of a mental property to an object of awareness on pain of a vicious infinite regress.

I conclude that the property of the state of consciousness that points to or is of or represents the object of awareness does so by its intrinsic nature, that it is a *natural* sign of what it represents and that states of consciousness are therefore a species of, and almost certainly the only species of, *natural representation*. But the argument from infinite regress can be generalized and separated from the context of what one knows about one's own states of consciousness in yet another argument for natural representation.

The *dialectical* argument is one only for the existence of natural representation and therefore, in the present context, only for the existence of that kind of property of every state of consciousness that grounds what a particular such state is a consciousness of, that is, the kind of property that I just called a natural sign. At one level the argument is very simple and goes as follows: if there is either conventional representation or quasi-natural representation, there also must be natural representation; for the existence of either conventional or quasi-natural representation presupposes the existence of natural representation. And because, uncontroversially, there exists conventional representation, it follows that there is natural representation. Furthermore, this natural representation is and must be of the kind that is just that of the connection of a state of consciousness to the object of that state of consciousness. Thus states of consciousness are or contain natural representation, that is, entities that by their intrinsic nature represent something else. While in *Natural Signs* I examined this argument mainly in connection with the view of the relation of mind to language, here I shall attend more closely to the infinite-regress aspect.[6]

The controlling features of the forms of representation to which this argument applies are, obviously, their being, in the cases of conventional representation and quasi-natural representation, *three-term* relations and, in the case of natural representation, a *two-term* relation. The argument is roughly analogous to an obvious one concerning spatial relations: no two things could be in the relation of *being-to-the-left-of* except relative to a third thing, thus making that relation a three-term relation, unless that third thing were in some two-term relation to each of the first two things. Similarly, no two things can be in the three-term

6   Addis, *Natural Signs*, 57–65.

relation of either conventional representation or quasi-natural representation unless the third term of that relation is in a two-term representing relation to each of the other two terms. Why is that? Do all three-term relations presuppose some relevant two-term relation? The answer to that question is surely in the affirmative, but it doesn't follow from that general truth alone that the two-term relation has to be the *same* relation or even, with some flexibility, the same kind of relation as the three-term relation, although it ordinarily will be. So while it will probably be granted that the three-term representing relation does presuppose *some* two-term relation or other between the "third" and each of the other two relata, it doesn't yet follow that it must be a two-term relation of representation. So let us look yet more closely at the matter.

The crucial point here is that a first thing, the word *apple*, can (conventionally) represent a second thing, an apple, to a third thing, a person, only if that person can be *aware* of both the word *apple* and the apple independently of this conventional representation of the latter by the former. And this does not require any prior knowledge or understanding of the first *as* a word or the second *as* an object of a certain kind but only that degree or kind of awareness that enables the child to pick out, however roughly and with whatever initial mistakes, a particular auditory item and connect it with a separate visual item. The vast mysteries of language learning and coordination of the senses in humans and what they presuppose about the nature of the human brain are only beginning to be unraveled. But we may be confident that, whatever future discoveries may uncover, in the sense that is relevant to the present argument, human babies, just like other forms of animal life down to whatever simple levels, have states of consciousness without language even though those states of consciousness are, in humans, necessary conditions for learning a language and other forms of conventional representation as well as, if there is any, quasi-natural representation. Learning a language is in turn a causally necessary condition for the existence of certain forms of consciousness, including many of those most important to human existence. But we must never allow ourselves to be deceived into believing that the very existence of consciousness itself, in any significant sense, depends on learning language and somehow therefore postdates that learning.

Suppose then that the child is able to be aware of both the word *apple* and the apple itself prior to learning that the former is, for certain humans, a conventional sign for the latter. Is this awareness of, say, the apple a two-term or a three-term representation? If it were three-term, involving not the word *apple* but some other representation, the same question would only arise once more: is the child's awareness of that "other" (and still the apple, too) such that the "other" represents the apple to the child a two-term or a three-term relation? It is evident that as long as it is insisted that the relation must be a three-term relation, we are launched on a regress that, if it is not terminated by a case of two-term representation, is an infinite regress and indeed a vicious infinite regress. For every awareness would presuppose an infinite number of awarenesses; and because awarenesses are events in time, that would presuppose an infinite number of discrete awarenesses in a finite amount of time, which is impossible. (I put it this way to contrast it with the quite plausible proposition that a person might have an infinite number of *beliefs*, for beliefs are not awarenesses but dispositions or capacities of a certain kind, thus requiring only that a person, like any object, be capable of realizing any one from an infinite set of *possible* "responses," which is neither impossible nor paradoxical.) One must therefore conclude that awareness itself is two-term, that an awareness is or contains an entity that intrinsically represents whatever it does represent.

We have come to the following conclusions: first, there is natural representation; second, states of consciousness, and probably states of consciousness alone, possess natural representation; third, natural representation by a state of consciousness is grounded in the exemplification by it of a (monadic) property—a natural sign—that intrinsically represents or intends what that state of consciousness is a consciousness of; and, fourth, every state of consciousness exemplifies another (monadic) property that grounds its being the mode of the state of consciousness that it is. Thus, for a person to have the state of consciousness of imagining that Sirius has ten planets (as you, the reader, are now doing) just is for that person to exemplify the mode property of *being-an-imagining* and the intentional property or natural sign of *being-of-Sirius's-having-ten-planets*.

The next step in the argument will be to examine states of consciousness in connection with time, keeping in mind that music is an art that above all (but not alone) involves time in its very essence.

5

Time and Sound

Music takes time; consciousness takes time. That is the heart of the matter, to be sure, but it is yet a long way from showing how these two facts come together to explain, in part, the idea the music *represents* possible states of consciousness.

More specifically, but still only metaphorically, we may say that in the nonmental realm, music is the "image" of consciousness, being that feature of the physical world that is most similar, in a fundamental respect, to consciousness itself. Some people, particularly those still dominated by nineteenth-century ideas of expression and especially the artists among them, may object to my characterizing music as "nonmental" and as part of the "physical" world. But I speak neutrally, as far as possible, and mean this only in the commonsense way that, while not denying in the least all of the multifarious ways in which our emotions, beliefs, values, intentions, knowledge, and much else enter into the creation, performance, study, appreciation, preservation, encouragement, and much else of music, music as performed is a public, intersubjective object that is neither a mind nor part of a mind. Music is indubitably a *product* of minds; but, like most artifacts, it is ontologically independent of them. We may agree in some measure with those artists who might say, vaguely, that the music is only that which is heard and interpreted by particular listeners, or with those philosophers who might be eager to invoke the so-called primary/secondary quality distinction thereby insisting, in both cases, that *sounds* (as contrasted with sound *waves*) are really

57

in the mind. But agree or not (and I don't—with either group), we still have the distinction between what is heard and the hearing of it and the fact that what is heard is not in any case literally a *constituent* of any state of consciousness, even if it is in some extended sense "mental." But I am now on the verge of anticipating matters that must await further preparation.

While in *Philosophy in a New Key* Langer gives little explicit attention to time and its importance for understanding either music in itself or in its relation to the emotions, in the later *Feeling and Form* the notion of time comes almost to dominate her theorizing about music. Indeed, the main chapter on music has the title "The Image of Time," and in it Langer, without going back on any part of the theory that music symbolizes the forms of the emotions, develops an account of how music also symbolizes, in a different sense, the passage of time. Relying on a philosophical theory according to which "actual" time is merely the succession of events while experienced time also involves "passage" and "motion," she tells us that "the semblance of this vital, experiential time is the primary illusion of music." (*FF*, 109). It *is* an illusion because music does not literally possess either passage or motion—auditory objects cannot *move*—but it nevertheless presents such passage that "is measurable only in terms of sensibilities, tensions, and emotions" (*FF*, 109), thus connecting this idea with the earlier theory.

Langer expresses her agreement with Henri Bergson that experienced time—"*la durée réelle*," not to be confused with the "actual time" of the physical world—cannot be conceptualized or symbolized *discursively*. But in holding that music (and, to a lesser extent, dance and other "occurrent" arts, as she calls the performing arts) can and do symbolize experienced time, Langer rejects Bergson's further claim that some aspects of reality cannot be conceptualized or symbolized at all as well as his broader thesis that symbolization is falsification. At the same time, she clarifies, in an obvious way, her own ineffability thesis about what language cannot and music can express. Thus does music become, on her account, the "image" of time.

In a rare point of contact between the presumed liberating clarities of twentieth-century analytic philosophy and the presumed pretentious vaguenesses of its contemporary continental counterpart (both as seen from the analytic side), one finds a rather surprising quantum of agreement of most of the former with some of the latter that while time in itself just is the relations of succession and simultaneity thus excluding

any absolute "nowness" or "presentness" in the world, time as experienced does have aspects that can give one a sense of "passage" or "motion" from the past to the future through the present. Yet these notions
of movement apply literally only to displacement in space. How this
can be and what to make of it are the sources of a sizable literature
among analytic philosophers of time from Russell to the present. Fortunately, for our purposes, we need not enter this still inadequately
comprehended realm to any great distance. At the same time, it will not
be possible altogether to escape philosophical discussion of time, just
because it is required in order to understand clearly the crucial property
that consciousness and music share uniquely. But we need go no further with Langer here.

We turn first, then, to the connection between consciousness and time.
One finds in the literature occasional speculation on some putatively
profound connection between the two but little success or even attempt
to explain what it is. Bergson and his continental contemporary Edmund
Husserl as well as the latter's student, Martin Heidegger, are three of the
very few who have had something to say on the topic, while among
analytic philosophers only Gustav Bergmann and a handful of others
have made some suggestions. In a chapter on the topic in *Natural Signs*,
I ventured some ideas aimed mainly at explicating the idea found especially among the existentialists but also in Collingwood and others that
the mind is not a "thing," is a "nothingness" (but, of course, not nothing
at all in the sense of the eliminative materialists), that it is lacking in substance or structure, and the like. Here my purposes are different, but it
will be to the point all the same to summarize some of my arguments and
findings there while expanding on others.

Consider then all the properties that are exemplified by particular
things, whether those particular things be thought of as *objects* such as
chairs and stars and human bodies or more as *events* or *states* such as taking walks or political revolutions or mental acts. That set of properties,
it would seem, can be divided into two exclusive and jointly exhaustive
subsets of such properties as follows: those properties that could be exemplified in a world without time, and those properties that require
time for their exemplification. The 'could' and 'require' here are, as one
says, *ontological* (some would say "logical") and not causal or otherwise
empirically contingent. That is, they have to do with the very natures
of the properties themselves and not with laws of nature or any other

contingent connections any properties happen to have. For examples, it seem obvious that the properties of *being-triangular* and *being-ten-meters-square* could be exemplified in a timeless, changeless universe and just as obvious that the properties of *being-a-revolution* and *being-a-birth* could be exemplified only in a universe of time and change.

Let us, for convenience, label any property that by its nature does require time for its exemplification a *T-property* (for "temporal") and any property that does not require time for its exemplification, that by its nature could be exemplified in a timeless world, an *N-property* (for "nontemporal"). Thus, while *being-triangular* is in fact exemplified only in this temporal world of ours, because it *could* exist in a nontemporal world, it is an N-property. And because *being-a-birth* requires a temporal world for it to be exemplified, it is a T-property. It is clear then that for any property of particular things and events we are acquainted with, whether by the outer senses or through introspection or bodily sensation or any other means including imagination, we can say that it is either a T-property or an N-property but never neither nor both.

Because the only properties we know directly are those exemplified in our temporal world, it is evident that our knowledge that a given property is a T-property or that it is an N-property is based not on observing worlds of the two kinds and thereby discovering which properties belong to which subset. Furthermore, because N-properties can be exemplified in both temporal and nontemporal worlds, proceeding in such a manner would require the further assumption that the nontemporal world one is observing (*per impossibile*) contains all the N-properties there are and that one is observing them. It would seem to follow that our knowledge of which properties belong to which kind is not based only, or even most importantly, on the observation of properties in their actual settings; for observation of those settings is manifestly insufficient to the knowledge that we in fact possess.

The only conclusion we can draw is that our knowledge of this kind is based on consideration of the natures of the properties themselves. Just by considering the nature of the property *being-triangular* we know that it could be exemplified in a timeless world, just as we know by considering the nature of *being-a-birth* that it could not be exemplified in a timeless world, that it requires time and change. One may say, if one likes, that "by definition" births can occur only in temporal worlds, but it is important to understand that these facts about the nature of properties have nothing whatsoever to do with language or the particularities of culture (in the anthropologists' sense) or indeed anything human or "subjective." It is we who can discover, by thinking about it, that *being-triangular* is an N-property, but we do not make it so by thinking it or knowing it; that is a fact about the property itself that derives from its (inherent) nature and nothing else.

Some philosophers balk at the idea of knowledge of this kind, believing (if they are not skeptics altogether) that there is always some further explanation, at least in principle, of why something is the case and that saying it is just the nature of the thing is, even if true, empty and trivial, perhaps just a way of saying that one doesn't know the real explanation. This essay is not a treatise in general epistemology or philosophy of science and I am in any case unprepared to mount a comprehensive defense of the possibility and nontriviality of knowledge of this kind. I will observe only, first, that all of us have knowledge of this kind, admit it or not; second, that much of what we uncontroversially do know (again, except for those who affect to be skeptics) would seem to presuppose knowledge of this kind; while, third, that to admit knowledge of this kind would seem to be indifferent to the usual issues of foundationalism and its alternatives in epistemology, falling as the kind of knowledge it is nearer the category of the *a priori* than the commonly empirical. One must know by experience what *being-triangular* is before one can acquire the further knowledge that it is an N-property, but that further knowledge would not seem to require more than holding the property before one's mind and considering its nature.

None of this, however, is to imply that we may not sometimes disagree in a particular case whether a given property is a T-property or an N-property or that, at the least, we shall have to think very hard, sometimes possibly with no deep conviction as to the result. How about the property, for example, of *being-a-book* or the property of *being-salty*? Much of this is, no doubt, a matter of discovering or, more likely, deciding exactly what property it is we are intending to pick out by our words or thoughts—whether, for example, we choose to include its causal history in what it is to be a book. And having made that choice, we may often proceed comfortably to the answer. In other cases, it may not be so easy just because we don't fully grasp the nature of the property that, all the same, we have succeeded in identifying.

We can now apply this distinction to the properties that characterize states of consciousness. In the last chapter I argued that a state of consciousness always has two properties that jointly make it just such a state—the one, a mode property, being a property that grounds the kind or mode of awareness that it is, the other, an intentional property, being a property that grounds its being of whatever it is of. I now submit the hypothesis, which is crucial to the ultimate theory I am developing about consciousness and music, that *mode properties and intentional properties are T-properties*. Consciousness can exist only in a temporal world. This is the important first step in understanding the connection between consciousness and time, and it needs, even in the present context of developing the larger and ultimate theory, considerable elaboration and defense.[1]

At one level, my argument and my appeal are simply to ask the reader to consider the nature of these properties (assuming that he or she has at least tentatively agreed that they exist and are the essential properties of states of consciousness) and to discover, as I claim to have discovered, that they are such that they could not be exemplified in a timeless world. But before I make a somewhat technical argument to the conclusion that the properties of states of consciousness *must* be T-properties, let us take note of the fact that when the maker of science-fiction movies wishes to portray a situation in which the world or some part of it is, so to speak, "frozen" and its inhabitants made changeless for some time (so the analogy is necessarily imperfect), the director invariably has those persons come out of their paralyses with no memory of the time during which they were "frozen." They are portrayed as continuing to have the usual bodily properties of shape and size and color and weight and so on, but with their consciousness having ceased existence. You can't "freeze" a state of consciousness. That's the way I would do it too, and I suggest that the movie maker's practice reflects the "intuitive" view that in a changeless world or situation, consciousness would not exist. But a timeless world is necessarily a changeless world even if, perhaps, the converse is not the case. Those movie makers have it right!

But there are considerations that go to the *ontological* heart of the matter having to do with the connection of *particularity* itself to space and time and that should convince anyone that states of consciousness can, in the ontological sense, exist only in a temporal world—anyone, that

---

[1]   One rather significant consequence of the present hypothesis is that the theological notion of a minded being who is "outside" time is the notion of something that is ontologically impossible.

is, who believes that the properties that characterize states of consciousness are a set of properties distinct from any that pertain to physical objects and events. The fundamental fact underlying these considerations is that a state of consciousness—my present imagining that Sirius has ten planets, for example—appears to the one who has that state to have no spatial location; our conscious states *seem* to be in time but not in space. We have become accustomed to thinking of our minds as having some very special connection with our brains, which assuredly do have spatial location; but we may well recall that not all peoples have believed that the "seat" of consciousness is in the head. And, more specifically, while neurologists may be able to tell us just what part of the brain was "involved" in, say, imagining that Sirius has ten planets, that particular state of consciousness, as one may be aware of it by introspection, is not, or at least is not given as being, where that brain state is or indeed in any particular location or even as having any location. It would seem that while every particular object and event is in time, only some but not all of them are in space. And it would seem further that to be a particular object or event requires, ontologically, being in space or time or both, partly for the reasons to follow.[2]

Many philosophers are quite uncomfortable with the idea of something that is particular and in time but not in space, and this is surely one of the motives if not an argument for maintaining that, whatever the testimony of introspection may suggest, states of consciousness are in fact in space, perhaps by way of being "identical" to certain states of the brain or other physical configurations. My argument is only—and it is all that is required—that a state of consciousness is given *as* particular, that is, as an event at a particular time, but not *as* having spatial location. Because at least this much is the case, its particularity as a state of consciousness cannot depend, ontologically, on its being in space even if it is in fact in space (which I see no good reason at all to believe). Instead, its particularity can depend only on its *duration*.

While what makes my desk a particular object is, primarily, its *extension* in space, what makes my imagining that Sirius has ten planets a particular something-or-other (not to beg the question by saying "event") can only be that it has a certain duration in time. To be sure, the

---

[2] This line of thought also would seem to entail that the notion of a particular being, whether minded or not, that is "outside" of space and time is the notion of something that is ontologically impossible.

desk also has a duration as well as an extension, and to be a physical object in our universe is indeed to have both features. But its particularity is secured by either feature alone, and our conception of a desk, especially our imaging of one, naturally turns to it as extended in space instead of stretching through time. But this is just another way of saying that while a desk (or a desk-slice, if you prefer) could exist in a timeless universe because the properties that define a desk as a desk are all N-properties, the properties that define a state of consciousness as a state of consciousness are, necessarily, T-properties. For the only thing that can ground the particularity of a state of consciousness is its duration in time and never its extension or location in space; either it has no extension or location in space or, if it does, it is not given as having either while its particularity is given.

We thus arrive at the conclusion that because a state of consciousness necessarily exists in its particularity only as a duration (or as something that necessarily has duration), its essential properties can only be of a kind that can be exemplified by what has duration. To be sure, this argument does not quite *formally* prove this conclusion insofar as it could conceivably be maintained that while, in our universe, any particular that exemplifies the essential mode property and the essential intentional property that makes it a state of consciousness exists only as, or as having, a duration, those properties themselves could be exemplified by a particular that exists only as, or as having, spatial extension. And here, perhaps we are at the end of argument, being faced with an appeal to the natures of the properties themselves. I say that a particular that is extended in space *could* not, in the ontological sense of the modal term, exemplify the essential properties of consciousness any more than a desk (or desk-slice) could do so. The various property compatibilities, necessary connections, and necessary exclusions have no further ontological ground than the natures of the properties themselves. So one may, if one wishes, regard the argument I have just made regarding the connection of particularity to space and time as ultimately, like my initial argument, an appeal to the natures of the properties themselves but here as calling attention to the necessary exclusivity of the essential properties of consciousness on the one hand and any properties that could be exemplified by a spatially extended or located particular on the other.

Descartes was right, after all, in insisting that mind and body are necessarily distinct, but still wrong in supposing that the mind is a *sub-*

stance and one that must always be in operation.[3] He was wrong also, as we must now understand clearly for my ultimate purposes, if he supposed that *all* physical (or nonmental) things are extended in space even if all such objects do have spatial location. He forgot about sounds!

Sounds have received very little attention from philosophers, probably on the false but initially plausible assumption that whatever philosophical interest they have is held in common with the materials of sight, the sense that, for most humans, is the primary one for getting about. Although the social world is heavily shaped and even, in some ways, constituted by sounds in the form of the artifactual component of spoken language, there has been little attempt to understand either just what sounds are, ontologically, or what role they do or could play in our knowledge and understanding of the world generally.[4]

A sound, while perhaps always produced by at least one object that has extension in space (it doesn't really matter here), is itself, at least sometimes, a particular object or event that has spatial location but no spatial extension. Is spatial location alone sufficient ontologically to secure an object's particularity? Another way of putting this question is to ask whether or not a sound could exist in a timeless universe. For if so, then neither duration nor extension is necessary for particularity. But the answer to the question, I submit, is obviously negative: sounds can exist only in a temporal world. To be a C-sharp, that is, an object or event with the property of *being-C-sharp*, is necessarily to have a duration (once more, when the maker of a science-fiction movie wishes to portray, however imperfectly, a situation without time or change that situation will as surely lack sounds as it lacks consciousness.)

(Whether or not a sound *can* be extended in space—my argument requiring only that none need be and that some are not—is a subtle question of ontology and phenomenology that, fortunately, we need not pursue. The reader will recall Langer's insistence that music presents only the "illusion" of motion and passage, suggesting that she probably doubted the possibility. But it is not clear whether she was referring to

[3] For my criticisms of the theory of mental substance, which are based on the idea that if there were such things they would have to have mental N-properties, see Addis, *Natural Signs*, 151–161.

[4] One exception—to my knowledge, virtually alone among analytic philosophers—is Peter Strawson, *Individuals: An Essay in Descriptive Metaphysics* (New York: Anchor, 1963), the chapter called "Sounds," in which he explores the implications of sounds being the only objects of sense experience, what he calls a "No-Space" world.

the purely aural characteristics themselves or to a sound as an object with a spatial location. Part of the problem here, as in many contexts involving the ontology of particularity, is what is to be regarded as *an* object or *an* event and whether or not there are absolutely simple objects and events; in short, whether or not, ontologically speaking, there is any objective basis for what counts as *a* particular. That there are causal bases and ones that rely on human needs and purposes is obvious when one gets beyond the phenomenologically simple. That is why much substance metaphysics, especially in its theories of forms or natures, errs in mistaking the causal and the cultural for the ontological.)

A sound, I insisted, like a state of consciousness requires duration for its existence. Sounds can exist only in a temporal world. It is important here to emphasize that I am, indeed, talking about sounds and not sound *waves*. That is, our subject is what we actually *hear* and not what the scientists tell us is the cause of what we hear. At this insistence many kinds of critics will want to object. Some will say that, conceived as different from sound waves, sounds simply don't exist; others will, perhaps reluctantly, grant their existence but only as being, contrary to my assumption, the same thing as sound waves; while yet a third group of critics will maintain both the existence and the difference of sound from sound waves but insist that these features entail that sounds are only "in" the mind.

These are mostly the same critics I confronted in the last chapter, where I suggested that, strictly speaking, music is a physical phenomenon; and my replies here are largely the same. Taking my critics in reverse order, I repeat that even if sounds are in some important sense "in" the mind, there remains the distinction between what is heard and the hearing of it; no sound is literally a *constituent* of a state of consciousness even if, as the critic maintains, a sound is *dependent* on a state of consciousness for its existence. To the reductionist who would identify sounds with sound waves I can say only what one should say in all such cases: the properties of the one are simply given to us as *different* from the properties of the other: a sound just isn't anything like its primary cause, the sound wave, any more than the tides are like their primary cause in the relative positions of Earth and moon. To those who deny the existence of sounds altogether, I have nothing, systematically speaking, to say, for there can be no genuine argument here. I can only repeat my principle that one should always take the world as one finds it, unless there are compelling reasons to do otherwise. And in the context of our present issue, no such reasons have ever been advanced.

Sounds require duration. Do they also require *change*? Here we must approach a question in the philosophy of time that once again shows the profound connection between particularity on the one hand and space and time on the other with its corollary of the strict ontological impossibility of a particular object or event that is "outside" space and time.

Particularity, we now appreciate, is intimately bound with extension in space and duration in time. Is it, as might be suggested, just the *same thing* as extension and duration; that is, is a particular just a "piece" of extension or of duration (or both)? The relevant alternative here is the theory that extension and duration are (monadic) properties that are exemplified by particulars, combined with the thesis that no particular can fail to exemplify the one or the other. This, I think, is one of most difficult questions of general ontology; and while it is initially attractive to many to suppose that a particular is a constituent of objects, facts, and events that, to speak with a certain tradition, "underlies" all of its features including those of spatial and temporal location, the intimacy we have noted suggests instead that particulars just *are* extensions and durations. And while it is easier to think of extensions as particulars than to regard durations as particulars, further reflection suggests that this in only a consequence of our spatially oriented minds, which, while more closely linked ontologically with time than space, are psychologically more prone to "spatialization": we find it easier to picture and to represent all manner of things, including the mathematical and the temporal and the mental, in geometrical terms than any other. This consequence can be overcome, as it were, by the considerations already advanced and the further point that by so regarding particulars, the question of whether or not we are "acquainted" with them seems to admit of an easy affirmative answer. But much murkiness remains in these matters, and the connections of particularity, duration, and consciousness may never be fully understood.

Enough has been established, however, to make plausible the thesis that, contrary to received opinion, *there can be time without change.* Change entails time, so to speak, but time does not entail change. Change involves some difference in the *distribution* of properties from one time to another in a way that would make qualitatively different *descriptions* apt for some point of a world from one moment to another. (So we exclude the so-called property of *being-older* and any other "property" that is entailed by the mere "passage" of time and that would be shared by all objects.) While the precise formulation of this idea is difficult if not impossible, its basic feature is entirely clear: such change may involve motion but it need not; change of color is an example of a change that does not, ontologically, involve motion. (Of course, motions of atoms and molecules are causally required for change of color as they are, so the physicists tell us, for every occurrence of any kind.) With or without motion, every change trivially but essentially involves time.

But can there really be time without change? Sounds that do not change their timbre or volume or pitch illustrate just that possibility. For a sound requires a duration yet may not involve any change (except, again, in the irrelevant causal sense). Indeed, it seems to be the case that, *alone among physical phenomena known to us, sounds require duration but do not require change*. Or to put the thesis a little more precisely: in the physical world, the only T-property that does not also require change is that of *being-a-sound* and whatever "other" properties sound involves such as timbre, pitch, and volume. The exemplification of any other T-property in the physical world such as *being-a-birth* or *being-a-revolution* requires not only duration but change as well.

If I am right, this gives sounds a very special ontological status in the physical realm. I don't know how to prove that this is so, for, by the nature of the situation, any "proof" would require taking every property one by one and showing that it doesn't have the crucial feature. So I can only ask the reader first to consider the nature of the property *being-a-sound* and then to try to think of some other physical property that shares this feature with that property. It is tempting to think of *being-a-light* or *being-a-color* or *being-a-taste*, as has been suggested to me; but further reflection shows, I believe, that each of these and every other initial candidate either is not a T-property at all or is one that requires change. With respect to the three just mentioned, it is important, as always, not to identify the property in question with the experience of it. The *experience* of saltiness, to take an example that may serve for all instances of these three generic properties, indeed is or involves T-properties. That is only because the experience is just that—a state of consciousness. Saltiness itself—the property ham has—is not a T-property but instead an N-property. So the issue of *its* involving time without change does not arise.

While the feature of requiring time but not change may be unique to sound in the physical world, it is not unique in reality as a whole: states of consciousness too are such as to require time but not change. I have already argued that states of consciousness can exist only in a temporal world, but I now further submit that a given state of consciousness, such as imagining that Sirius has ten planets, is an occurrence that involves time but not change. There is just the simultaneous exemplification by a particular that is a duration of the mode property of *being-an-imagining* and of the intentional property (natural sign) of *being-of-Sirius's-having-ten-planets*, both of which are T-properties. There is no good reason at all to suppose that either a mode property or an intentional property is such that it involves change through time and so no good reason to suppose that a state of consciousness requires such change. Yet it requires time itself. (How much time is required, the temporal length of what psychologists call "the specious present," is of no moment here, but it is at most a few seconds. Of course, one can think of or perceive the same thing over much longer periods of time, but this involves a *succession* of momentary states of consciousness of similar, even exactly similar, properties.)

My conclusion is by now obvious and can be stated very briefly: *states of consciousness and sounds alone are such that, while they require time for their existence, they do not require change.* This ontological affinity of consciousness and sound that sets them apart from everything else in this crucial regard suggests that, so to speak, consciousness might find in sound an "image" of itself not merely in the feature that we have just identified but in more complicated ways as well. This is the germ of the main thesis of this essay, that *music represents possible states of consciousness*; and we are now prepared, with understanding of its ontological ground, to pursue this idea in more detail.

6

The New Theory

In this chapter I set out the new theory. The defense of the theory will be twofold: first, to show that the theory is *possibly true* in being both internally coherent and consistent with all the relevant facts about music and people; and second, to argue that the theory is the *best explanation* of certain of those same facts about music and people and in particular of the somewhat vague but universally known fact that consists of the power and attraction music has for human beings.

This new theory of the relation of music to the emotions and certain other conscious states retains all three of the fundamental features of Susanne Langer's: isomorphism, representation, and ineffability. It rests on the ontological affinity of consciousness and sound that was revealed in the preceding chapter and on the idea of quasi-natural representation that was developed in Chapter 3. Furthermore (in an aspect of my account that for some will cast the whole theory into immediate doubt), I not only do not assert but instead emphatically deny that the composer of music is ordinarily aware of these three fundamental features, and I reject as irrelevant entirely what the composer is "trying" to achieve and indeed anything at all about what went on in the composer's mind at the time of composition or any other time. For the purposes of my theory, it simply doesn't matter how the music came into existence. At the same time, among the relevant data to be explained by the theory is the fact that some people choose to be composers, a form

70

of life that is often very difficult with few of the rewards that matter to most people; for that fact is part of the vague fact mentioned above about the power music has for human beings.

Peter Kivy concludes his *Sound Sentiment* with the following challenge:

> Whenever I re-read *The Corded Shell* [an earlier book of Kivy's], I am convinced by my own arguments. Whenever I listen to a piece of complex expressive music, I am convinced that neither I nor anyone else understands how it is possible for the expressiveness to be in the music at all. It is there: of that I am sure; but how, in what manner remains to me a divine mystery. . . . I . . . see it as a question whose answer must be bounded by what I consider as the inviolable "purity" of pure instrumental music. It is particularly easy for philosophers, who have cleverness and ingenuity bred in the bone, to come up with intriguing explanations of musical expressiveness that, in the end, reduce pure music to some form of representation or emotive fiction. Indeed, since it is as yet unclear just why we should have any deeply abiding interest in the purely sensuous, syntactic, and formal structure of musical sound, we are often told, with evangelical fervor, that to view music as such trivializes it, and makes our enthusiasm for it unintelligible. This self-righteous attitude simply begs the most important question at issue. As philosophers of art, we must take it as a given datum that human beings *do* have a deep, emotional, and abiding interest in pure musical syntax and structure. This is a datum to be explained, not explained away. And until we explain it, there remains something mysteriously intriguing and deeply puzzling about human nature. (*SS*. 258–259)

Kivy has made his own attempt further to dispel the mystery in his subsequent *Music Alone* and *The Fine Art of Repetition* and elsewhere. While agreeing with most of the "sentiments" of his complaint and his charge, I must suggest that Kivy's contrast between the notion of representation on the one hand and that of our interest in the inherent features of the music as present especially in the case of pure instrumental music is itself question-begging: my new theory purports to explain our interest in the music itself in part by the fact that, unknown to the conscious mind for the most part, the listener is being represented to by the music. To what extent I will have succeeded myself in helping to dissipate the "divine mystery" (and with what degree of self-righteousness) will be for the reader to judge.

Here, then is a brief statement of the theory: passages of music are *isomorphic* with certain possible states of consciousness. While music may also be, almost surely is, isomorphic with other actual and possible events and states of affairs, because consciousness and sound have a profound ontological affinity with respect to time and because human nature is what it is, music is a quasi-natural *representation* of possible states of consciousness to human beings such that, at some level of awareness that is not ordinarily that of what one is attending to, we are presented with those possible states of consciousness by music; that is, music *brings them to mind,* if not always to the conscious mind. Finally, certain subtle differences in both the intentions and especially the modes of states of consciousness that are *ineffable,* that is, cannot be captured in language, can be represented to us by music; where language fails, music can sometimes succeed in symbolizing to us the nuances of mood and other aspects of consciousness.

These three features together, and to some extent singly, are intended to account for the power music has for us: there is a unique isomorphism between music and the emotions that allows the latter to be represented to us by music and in a way that other symbolic systems, including language, cannot do. Our human nature is involved both as what makes possible our being represented to by sounds of a certain kind and as what is itself partially revealed to us by music beyond the uncontroversial sense—that music is a human product. It is a human product—we compose it, perform it, and listen to it—just because of its connection to our nature in the nontrivial senses.

It is clear that it is the feature of representation that is the heart of the matter. If I am right, it is the unique isomorphism that makes the representation possible; but by itself, as so many commentators have noted, isomorphism explains nothing about the power of music. And while the ineffability thesis adds to the explanation of music's power, it is logically independent of the isomorphism/representation part of the theory and could, therefore, be dispensed with while retaining a theory that would still explain music's hold on us. (In any case, the ineffability thesis is, strictly speaking, one about *language,* not music. For what music can do is itself logically independent of what language can and cannot do. But I shall continue to use the idea of ineffability to mean that music can represent some differences that language cannot. So it adds to the explanation only in the weak sense that we turn to music for the expression of certain things that language cannot express.)

Let us now look into the matter of isomorphism in more detail. The isomorphism of music and states of consciousness is one of both form and content. While it may be the case, with Langer, that the physiological accompaniments of emotion (which she seems almost to identify with the forms of the emotions) are represented by music; and the case, with Kivy, that the behavioral expressions of emotions in humans are represented by music (in both cases through resemblance), the fundamental representation that takes place with music is the representation of the form and the content of states of consciousness, especially the having of emotions, themselves. It is fundamental in that it is this representation that is the explanation of the power of music and also in the sense that all music, indeed all sound, does represent in some measure. In this sense, what sets music apart from other sounds is only a matter of degree; and this, to my way of thinking, is as it should be. This consequence of the new theory in no manner diminishes the significance of the achievements in the composition of music any more than the fact that many nonpaintings have colors and shapes that may affect us or in which we see representations diminishes the importance of the achievements of painters. But this is another variation of one of my subthemes —that in general, for the purposes of understanding works of art, as contrasted with understanding the creators of artworks, what matters is the nature of what was created and not how it was created.

Music has form and music has content; and while it is not easy to specify the exact nature of this distinction, it is incumbent on me at least to indicate what differences I am referring to in the cases of both music and consciousness. As for music, it is common with respect to form to make some distinction between the form that is perceived by hearing the music performed and the form that is discovered only by analysis of the score. Musical forms have to do with matters of repetition and resemblance—of pitches, of relative pitches (as in the case of a melody repeated a fifth higher, for one kind of example), of rhythms, even of texture and dynamics (volumes of pitches), and much more. Classically, we think of the forms of Western art music as what is denoted by such expressions as "sonata-allegro," "rondo," "theme and variations," "trio," and so on—forms that usually can be heard and reported on by the reasonably educated listener. I have heard a distinguished contemporary

American composer insist that "whatever can be conceived can be perceived" in music, meaning perhaps that, in principle, someone or other is able to come eventually to discern by hearing any aspect of form that a piece of music might possess. But it is generally agreed, sometimes disapprovingly, that in much twentieth-century Western art music, many aspects of form are not perceivable as such, especially in those compositions whose forms reside partly in precise "mathematical" relationships (as some composers like to call them when they have deliberately constructed them, even though all music has them); for example, each section of a piece being exactly twenty-five percent longer than the immediately preceding section.

Part of the issue here has to do with the meaning of the word 'perceive' itself, and I have so far been rather casual in my own use, especially for a philosopher. To illustrate just some of the complications: we say that a person can perceive a chiliagon and indeed each of its thousand sides, but one can't perceive it *as* a chiliagon, at least not without prior knowledge, in the sense of being able to tell by perceiving it "as a whole" that it is a chiliagon and not of some more or fewer sides. Of course one can count up the sides by perception, somewhat as one can study a score by perception or replay a tape with a stopwatch and in those ways, which are also perceptual, determine the relevant properties. Yet these complications are, for the most part, irrelevant to my theory. For it is my claim that, *consciously perceived or not*, the forms of music present aspects of consciousness to us and have their effect on our responses to, and understanding of, the music. Thus, for the purposes relevant to the new theory, we have quite a liberal notion of the form of music.

Form is contrasted with content, and the standard view is that whereas Western art music of the Baroque and Classical eras emphasized form, the music of the Romantic era emphasized content (or "idea," as it is sometimes called in music as elsewhere), while the music of the twentieth century is, presumably, a hodge-podge, taken in the aggregate. Be all that as it may, content has to do with the "melodies" themselves, harmonies themselves, texture and dynamics themselves, rhythms themselves, and much more—in short, everything that form has to do with but considered not as repeated or resembling or in any other relation to other parts or aspect of the music. Put this way, the distinction between form and content is, needless to say, far too rigidly drawn insofar as each invariably contributes in some measure to the other, but for our analytic purposes it will suffice. To put it very roughly, we may say that to place emphasis on content is for the composer to stress the present moment (although, again, it is the music itself and not the composer's intentions that we are literally talking about), possibly at the expense of the form. But these are irremediably vague matters and few composers would admit to, or even recognize themselves as heeding, the call to stress the one at the expense of the other. It is to be noted however that while it makes perfect sense to talk about the form of, say, a particular chord in terms of its constituent pitches and other aspects, in general the form of an entire piece of music has to do with matters of repetition, resemblance, and other relations over longer periods of time.

Similarly, while one can talk about the "form" of a particular state of consciousness in terms of its possession of the two kinds of properties, the form of an emotion in the sense that is relevant to the new theory has much more to do with its longer extension in time and in particular with its subtle changes through time, in most cases. The content of a state of consciousness obviously just is the particular mode property and the particular intentional property that the state exemplifies.

But my thesis does not, in any case, either affirm or require a simple isomorphism between, on the one hand, what are usually regarded as the forms of music and what, in a stretched use, may be called the "forms" of consciousness or of emotion (or mood or sensation) and, on the other hand, between the contents of music and the contents of states of consciousness. Neither conventional signs nor natural signs have any significant isomorphism of that kind with what they are signs of despite the claim that "the form of the fact must be shared with the form of the proposition" and the idea of "one name/one thing" in the philosophical notion of an ideal language. The quasi-natural signs that music contains on my account present to us those states of consciousness that are the having of emotions, the being in certain moods, the awareness of sensations, and (possibly) other kinds of awarenesses. Music does so by having the forms and contents it does have and it presents both the forms and the contents of those kinds of states of consciousness. But it does not do so by the fact—because it is not a fact—that there is a simple correlation of the elements of the music to the elements of those states of consciousness, where "elements" are themselves both form and content of both music and consciousness. In what then lies the isomorphism beyond the general fact that ties consciousness to sound such that only they can exist in temporal but changeless world?

The answer, empty and trivial though it may seem, is this: whatever isomorphism of music and those states of consciousness is required or in fact exists such that the one is a quasi-natural sign of the other. What one would like to be able to do, in defense of any form of a representative theory of music, is to specify a mapping of discrete aspects of music onto those of the relevant states of consciousness or, at least, to indicate a procedure for doing so. This, of course, cannot be done; and the impossibility of doing so is for some a strong consideration against the representative theory itself. It would be well to keep in mind in this matter, however, that such a mapping is not possible with thought itself, even if there exists, in any significant sense, a "language of thought."[1]

More to the point here is that on my form of the representative theory, the fundamental connections involved in the representation *to* humans *of* certain states of consciousness *by* music is *lawful*. That is the very notion of a quasi-natural sign, for reference to the *natures* of the entities involved—sounds and minds, the latter as both that which is represented and that to which the representation takes place—is ultimately to be understood by way of capacities to enter into certain lawful connections. Does a connection which is such that, by certain laws of nature, certain sounds and complexes of sounds considered in all their qualities present certain states of mind to humans who listen to those sounds presuppose some kind of isomorphism between those sounds and those states of mind? It seems clear to me that it does and so I have assumed. But its rigidity or lack thereof and its degree of specificity remain, and perhaps must remain, obscure.

Thus, if someone wishes to argue that there is really little to be said about the specific character of the isomorphism, I shall not protest. But it is important to understand that my version of the representative theory requires no more isomorphism than is required by any theory of any kind that maintains a systematic lawful connection between two sets of variables. Isomorphism is only the derivative notion, lawful connection the fundamental. And that, once more, when it also involves the idea of representation, is the very notion of a quasi-natural sign.

Quasi-natural representations, we recall, are such that their having the representative function they do have depends on the natures of all three

---

[1]   My theory of natural signs, with the theories of Chomsky and Fodor, has been so characterized in Dale Jacquette, *Philosophy of Mind* (Englewood Cliffs, N.J.: Prentice Hall, 1994), 105. I would not have made this categorization myself, and Jacquette does note that I explicitly endorse the primacy of thought to language.

terms of the representing relation: in this case music, certain states of consciousness, and human nature as characterized by the structure and composition of the human brain. Music is, therefore, usefully conceived as being "between" language and thought in its intentionality. On the one hand, while language is purely conventional in many of its aspects, and consciousness is natural in its intentionality, music like language requires a "third" in order for the representation to take place; on the other hand, music achieves this affect largely independent of human choice and will, as does consciousness itself. In another sense, however, music as it were stands "outside" both language and thought and nearer dreams and the symbols of ritual and religion in that, like them, we are not ordinarily consciously aware of what is being presented to us even though we are profoundly affected by the fact of the symbolism.

Music is, moreover, more like language than thought in another important sense: just as there are different languages, so there are different musical styles and traditions; and in order effectively to be represented to by a piece of music, one must "know" the style. Thus the degree to which one is actually represented to by a particular piece of music (putting aside all matters of concentration due to health, energy, hearing, worries, concern for the performers, and other distractions) will depend not only on the fact that one is a human being with a brain of a certain structure but also on one's previous experience and especially that kind of experience that just is coming to be familiar with a particular musical style. Style refers here not only to what constitutes the difference between, say, European-American art music and the art music of India but also, within European-American art music, the difference between, say, the late Romantic style of Gustav Mahler and the terse, expressionist style of the mature Anton Webern.

Just as there seem to be linguistic universals that, because of the structure of the human brain, greatly limit the range of the possible structures of human languages, so there are musical universals that, also because of the structure of the human brain *and* the natures of sound and consciousness, limit the range of possible structures of sounds that will in fact represent certain states of consciousness to human beings. It is clear then that the theory that music is a quasi-natural representation of certain states of consciousness does not exclude an important role for learning and experience in coming to know a musical style or tradition and so to become such that one is more fully represented to by the music of a style one has come to know. Coming to know the music of another

culture (I do not necessarily mean culture in the geographical sense) is
indeed a way of coming to know, at some level, the kinds of inner states
that the members of that culture can conceive and probably also have;
but the best music of some cultures, and therefore the best music of any,
is that music that presents to the listeners states of consciousness that are
only approximated in reality just because of their subtlety, complexity,
and refinement.[2] They are more to be appreciated than felt. That is why,
at least for some of us, music sometimes does seem to transport us to
another world—a very distinct experience for those who have it—in
which, paradoxically, a suspension of time seems to be combined with
awareness of certain kinds of states of consciousness that are not felt or
encountered in real life. I can report such an experience, for an example,
in listening to Arnold Schoenberg's *Five Orchestral Pieces*, especially the
movement called *Farben*. The best explanation of such experiences, I
submit, is to be found in the theory before us.

Why, it may well be asked, should it be just those inner states of emotion, mood, and sensation that music represents and not some or all
other states of consciousness including perceiving, doubting, imagining, and so on? I am not completely certain that music is in fact limited
to those forms of consciousness that come under the general heading of
"feeling" (but not, of course, in the literal sense of kinaesthetic awareness), that is, of emotion, mood, and sensation. But I can offer some
speculation about a connection at the physiological level between music and feeling that may have something to do with the matter.

As Julian Jaynes, in his provocative hypothesis about the origin of
consciousness (really *self*-consciousness, as I would call it), reports,
music is primarily a product of, and attended to as music by, the right
hemisphere of the human brain while language is primarily a left-
hemisphere phenomenon.[3] This is said to be true of the heavy majority

---

[2] I am even tempted to say that certain musical works fundamentally alter our "sensibilities," to take a convenient word from the literary world. These works present us with
moods, emotions, and other frames of mind that, as far as we know, have never been experienced or even conceived, but that may come partially to define a culture. In that
sense—vague, to be sure—one might understand Beethoven's Third Symphony as a fundamental event in Western and, eventually, world civilization. No work of our century,
which we commonly think of as containing a more decisive break with the compositional
tradition, marks such an innovation in the representation of the inner life as the *Eroica*, although Stravinsky's *Le Sacre du Printemps* and Schoenberg's *Five Orchestral Pieces* may be
regarded in a similar vein.

[3] Julian Jaynes, *The Origin of Consciousness in the Breakdown of the Bicameral Mind* (Boston:
Houghton Mifflin, 1976), the chapter called "Poetry and Music."

of right-handed people and a significant percentage of left-handed people. Citing studies (and there are probably many more since the publication of his book) that show that damage to the relevant hemisphere can destroy either one's capacity for speech or one's capacity for music while preserving the other intact, Jaynes reasons that music, like poetry (but not in the sense of speech), originates in that part of the brain that, on his theory, was originally the seeming voice of the gods in our hallucinating ancestors and that remains the "voice" of the muses in their nonhallucinating descendants. The Greek *mousikē technē* was originally any art over which the Muses presided, but came later to refer only to that art—music—in which, as some report, the artist may have a particularly intense feeling of being "merely" the means by which the Muses speak (so to speak).

The phenomenon, familiar to creative people in many domains including philosophy and science, of seeming to be merely a *means* by which something—an artwork, a philosophical or scientific theory, a way of doing something—comes into existence instead of being simply its creator (though not, of course, without causal antecedents) would seem to derive from the fact, if I may so put it, that whereas the sense of self and of control is primarily located in the left hemisphere, creativity in general is to be found in the right hemisphere. What comes from the right hemisphere therefore sometimes has that character of not being one's own. In the extreme case of the schizophrenic, the products of the right hemisphere not only seem to be but are taken actually to be the voices of others, this being, on Jaynes's theory, also the case with our not very distant ancestors even if, according to him, they did not endure the suffering of modern schizophrenics.

The fundamental point here is that music—in its creation, performance, appreciation, and understanding—is primarily a right-hemisphere enterprise although, needless to say, many aspects of music including theory, history, facets of composition and performance, and much more involve the analytic and critical skills that derive from the left hemisphere. But music *as music*—that is, as sounds that are produced and heard in a certain way—is mainly right-hemisphere.

It remains, in this speculation about why music has to do especially with emotion, mood, and sensation, to point out that they, too, are right-hemisphere forms of awareness while the more cognitive forms are primarily left-hemisphere. That is why, I hesitatingly suggest, at the physiological level music represents only certain kinds of states of awareness and not certain other kinds. And that is why, too, the performance of music can serve so well as a means by which a performer can express his or her feelings just because it presents certain feelings to us by being their quasi-natural representation.[4]

Music, being the "language" of emotion, mood, and sensation in the sense of being a representation of them, does not, on my account, *assert* anything about them or anything else. In that sense, it would be much better to say that passages and pieces of music are aural "depictions" of the emotions and not descriptions, just as some paintings are depictions of landscapes without being descriptions of them. Depictions don't assert anything; they just depict. As such, they are neither true nor false, for in picturing something the issue of the reality of what is pictured is not involved, analytically speaking. One may ask the question, to be sure, but it is neither raised nor inadvertently answered *as such* by the depiction. I say "as such" because the awareness of anything whatsoever may be a source of knowledge, and if music does not assert anything about the emotions because it doesn't assert at all, it may yet enable us to find out something about the emotions by way of being a representation of them, that is, bringing them to mind. Nor does this require that we be consciously aware of music as such a representation in order to gain such knowledge, for we come to know many things about the world without being consciously aware of how we came to such knowledge or even that we possess it.

In particular, I want to maintain that music presents to us and makes it possible for us to come to know (if only while the music is being heard, according to Langer) aspects of and especially subtle differences of and among the emotions, moods, and sensations that language can only much less perfectly describe. Just as a picture can better depict a landscape than language can describe it, so music can better "depict" an

---

[4]   But I am not suggesting that any such feelings in the performer are, analytically, either a necessary or a sufficient condition for music to be such a representation. On the purely causal side, the professional musician is more often than not called upon to produce a representation of feelings that he or she utterly lacks at the moment and perhaps any moment, even if some pedagogues—in music as in other of the performing arts and especially acting—teach that the performer "must" or should try to feel the emotions that he or she is trying to "express." It remains the case that we often use our voices and musical instruments for the conscious purpose—often in solitude—of expressing our feelings, sometimes with the hope or intention of changing those feelings, just as any activity might be so used.

emotion than language can describe it. More than that: just as even a language so rich in its adjectives as English must fall short in describing what some pictures can depict—consider, for example, Rembrandt's self-portraits even as restricted to his purely physical characteristics—so must it fall short in describing what some music can "depict." This is my form of the ineffability thesis with its complement of the capacity of music to represent some aspects of reality—including what is possible but not actual—that language cannot. It is not, as Langer's view seems to be, that what is "depicted" by music—the emotions or, more precisely, the having of the emotions—is of a logical form that sentences of natural language are unable to express. I don't really quite understand what this could mean in any literal sense: the emotions and the having of the emotions are, by my way of thinking, the exemplification by certain particulars of certain properties and relations and as such are part of our "subject/predicate" world like all other facts and states of affairs, actual and possible.[5]

My ineffability thesis has to do only with the properties that are involved in those actual and possible states of affairs that just are the having of emotions, mood, and sensations. The idea is that there are an infinite number of such properties that, in many dimensions, form a so-called dense continuum but for which, because of the natures of the properties involved, there can be no "algorithm of naming," so to speak, (unlike certain series of numbers, for example). That is not to say that music can do the job fully either, that is, capture every possible difference of emotion, mood, and sensation, but only that music can and does capture some differences that language cannot. There is nothing in the least mysterious or unintelligible in this idea, at least on the side of the inadequacies of language; and I think we all recognize, when we think about it, that some other kinds of artifacts often do a far better job than language in representing certain features of reality and possibility to us, these artifacts including blueprints and maps, graphs and charts, gestures and artworks.

In the next chapter I shall discuss the general matter of what it is, how it is possible, and evidence for its actuality of our being represented to without conscious awareness of it. I end this chapter with discussion of

---

[5] In "The Ontology of Emotion," I offer a theory as to just what kind of particulars and just what kinds of properties and relations are in involved in emotions and the having of emotions.

the somewhat related matter, raised by Kivy in the passage from *Sound Sentiment* quoted earlier, of why it is, on any theory that holds music to be a kind of representation, it is the music itself to which we attend and which arrests us in listening to it.

One could almost say, I believe, that to be an artwork just is to be the sort of object or event that both symbolizes something and that is of interest in itself. Certainly there is no doubt, nor could Kivy possibly be thinking otherwise, that some artworks do represent something else and yet are such that the artwork itself and not what it represents is the main object of interest and attention for the listener or viewer or reader. The case of painting is probably the clearest and least controversial, although the precise "phenomenology" of the situation, which in any case varies from viewer to viewer and within a single viewer from occasion to occasion if not moment to moment, is not easy to describe (more ineffability, perhaps). As one looks at a Rembrandt self-portrait, it is obviously the painting and not Rembrandt one is perceiving in the literal sense; but the painting does indeed present Rembrandt to the viewer by way of depicting him. And when one knows who the subject of the painting is, one's conscious attention is undoubtedly of both the painting and what the painting represents. Even if one does not know who the subject is in particular, if indeed it is anyone in particular, one is still aware of someone depicted as well as the depiction of him or her.

Why then is one interested in the painting itself as an artwork? Perhaps the question as posed almost answers itself: there are many reasons a person might be interested in the painting, but from the aesthetic point of view they may include admiration for the skill and originality of the depiction, awareness of its status as an artifact intended to be viewed for its own sake, and pleasure in the organization of the materials of shape and color. There really is no particular mystery as to why, if something is a symbol, we can or should be interested in, and perhaps consciously attend to, both symbol and symbolized.

Susanne Langer, while possibly herself sometimes wrongly transporting features of symbolization in language to the arts, warned against thinking of language as the paradigm of symbolization. The use of language is no more (and probably no less) distinctively human among life forms of this planet than the creation, display, and appreciation of artworks. If one takes language as the paradigm, one is indeed tempted to suppose that the nature of the symbol is largely irrelevant, in the sense that as we read or talk or listen, we typically attend to what is being written or spoken about and not the words themselves. Needless to say, there are contexts in which the words themselves, as sounds or inscriptions, are of interest. The precise characterization of this fact is not possible but is adequately illustrated for our purposes by noticing that we sometimes can't remember whether we read about or were told about some matter even though the sounds of speech are, by any measure, quite unlike inscriptions and don't even involve the same organ of perception. One is no doubt less likely to forget whether it was a painting or a written description that gave one knowledge of a certain place, although many people will have had my own experience of forgetting, at least momentarily, whether it was by seeing a movie or reading a book that I know a certain story from some years ago.

But even in the case of language, as just noted, there are contexts—scientific and aesthetic—in which we attend to, have interest in, and take pleasure in the sounds or looks of words and sentences, in their organization, in the use of this word instead of that one, and so on. While the scientific study of words as objects may largely dissociate them from their meanings, hardly the same can be said of the appreciation of poetry, in which the word as object and the word as symbol are both essential. It is simply a mistake, I submit, to suppose that because something is a symbol, there arises a problem of why we should be interested in or take pleasure in our awareness of that symbol instead of attending only to what it symbolizes.

Peter Kivy's worry is therefore misplaced. Our "deep, emotional, and abiding interest in pure musical syntax and structure" excludes neither the possibility that music represents something that is not music nor, perhaps more to the point, the possibility that such representation is part of the explanation of the interest. Yet, to be sure, in the case of music we are not consciously aware, ordinarily, of the fact of such representation. To this as yet mysterious and seemingly paradoxical idea I now turn.

7

Unconscious Awareness

It is a curious fact, revealing the immense human capacity for self-deception about even the epistemologically most intimate matters that are not adequately reflected on, how extensive is the belief that a piece of music is sad just by virtue of its capacity to cause sadness in the listener. In my experience as a teacher I find, however, that students are easily disabused of this theory, a version of what I called the "listener-causal" theory, as well as its analogue version of the "composer-causal" theory. In the first case I have only to ask the students to reflect on their own experience as listeners and to report to them my own; in the other case I ask them to consider the fact that a composer may well feel happiness and excitement at the thought of the commission that he or she is about to receive while writing the agreed-upon sad piece of music.

That the composer sometimes is consciously *in mind of* sadness while composing the sad piece of music need not be denied, although being in such a state is neither logically nor possibly even causally necessary for success in doing so. Much more important for our concerns, that the listener sometimes is put *in mind of* sadness while listening to a sad piece of music *must* not be denied; for it is this fact above all that both is to be explained by the new theory and that in turn largely explains how it is that we do commonly apply the crucial predicates of emotion and sensation and mood to the music itself. (I described this complex fact earlier by saying that the phenomenological fact undergirds the anthropological fact.) The question, once again, is just how music does put a listener in mind of certain states of consciousness and in other ways affect him or her; and my answer, once again, is that does so by presenting those states of consciousness to the listener by way of being their quasi-natural representations.

In this chapter, I propose to answer the question of how a representation can take place without conscious awareness of it. What could such a representation be? And assuming that one can make sense of the notion in general, what evidence could there be and what evidence is there that such representations are actually taking place in the case of music and states of consciousness?

Langer herself noted that there is a certain similarity between the idea of symbolism in the arts in which the listener or viewer or reader, while being symbolized to, need not be consciously aware of that fact and certain theories of Sigmund Freud and Emile Durkheim that seem also to require such "unconscious" symbolism.[1] In Freud's case, the idea arises most interestingly in connection with his theory of dreams; in the case of Durkheim (but also in Freud), it is in connection with his theory of certain forms of religious belief and ritual. Exploration of these theories, or more exactly of what is presupposed by them even though not formulated or even clearly conceived by their founders, will be helpful to understanding the sense in which it may be said, truly or not, that music represents certain states of consciousness. Langer herself did not undertake this exploration, nor it seems did Freud or Durkheim or anyone else.

Before turning to a discussion of Freud and Durkheim directly, I want to call attention to a distinction that poses an important disanalogy between the symbolism that Freud and Durkheim find in dreams and religious beliefs respectively and the representation that, as I hold, obtains in listening to music. The distinction can be formulated as the difference between (1) a person's not being consciously aware of some state of affairs even though that state of affairs is being represented to that person, and (2) a person's not being consciously aware that something in particular is representing a certain state of affairs to that person

---

[1] Susanne Langer, *Philosophy in a New Key*, 38 and 177 on Freud and 50–51 on Durkheim. See also Langer, *Feeling and Form*, 239–243.

whether or not that person is otherwise consciously aware of that state of affairs.[2] The first no doubt better captures what Freud and Durkheim are about while the second better captures my idea of what goes on in listening to music. And it is clear that they are distinct if only because a person might be consciously aware of something without knowing what it is that has symbolized (or represented) that something to him or her, thus satisfying the second but not the first. But what the two propositions have in common is the notion of an unconscious awareness of some state of affairs, even if the second allows *also*—and not instead of—conscious awareness of that same state of affairs. Because this common element is the heart of the matter, I judge it to be valuable to proceed by discussion of Freud and Durkheim on symbolism.

Freud's work on dreams, even considered apart from its role in psychoanalysis, remains important today. The basic theory is set out in his massive *Interpretation of Dreams* published 1900. Its heart, as every likely reader knows, has to do with the contents of dreams and their connections with certain wishes, wishes that are said to be repressed while being sexual and infantile in origin. These connections, according to Freud's theory, are twofold: first, every dream is the *effect* of a wish of the described kind, that is, every dream is *caused by* a repressed, sexual, infantile wish; and second, every dream in its contents *symbolizes* (or "displays" or "represents") the wish that is its cause, in a more or less disguised form. It is, obviously, the second thesis that is of interest to us here and indeed only a part of that; namely, the part that says that the dream contents symbolize something or other, such symbolization taking place without conscious awareness of the dreamer either while dreaming or, ordinarily, otherwise.

It is crucially important to grasp, as Grünbaum points out in a recent critique of Freud's dream theory, that these two theses are logically independent of one another, for cause and content are themselves logically distinct.[3] That is, they are logically distinct unless the causal theory of content is true—the theory that to have a certain content in one's state of consciousness, whether it be a dream or a waking memory or

[2]   I am grateful to a reviewer who is unknown to me for calling attention to this important distinction.
[3]   Adolf Grünbaum, *Validation in the Clinical Theory of Psychoanalysis: A Study in the Philosophy of Psychoanalysis* (Madison: International Universities Press, 1993), 357.

whatever, just is to be in a state that has been caused in a certain way. We encountered this theory earlier in connection with general theories about the contents of states of consciousness, and rejected it. More important here, Freud himself clearly held cause and content to be logically distinct, and his theory of symbolism in dreams would be far less interesting were it to be reduced to a theory only about the causes of dreams. (It is clear, I trust, that what I am calling "content" is what Freud referred to as the "manifest content" of the dream—the dream as experienced or remembered by the dreamer—in contrast to what, according to the theory, is symbolized by the manifest content, which Freud unfortunately labeled the "latent content.")

There thus arises the question of what it is for a dream content to symbolize something of which the dreamer is not conscious.

One might suppose that if Freud himself had not already answered this question, surely some of his followers or critics would have done so. As far as I have been able to discover, neither Freud nor any of his commentators has even raised the question seriously, although its answer would seem to be essential to the very intelligibility of the theory. Granted that many notions are always simply assumed—for example, those of logic and mathematics in the work of empirical science—and rightly so, for there cannot be any absolutely presuppositionless inquiry, and granted too that one would not expect Freud to raise the philosophical question of the nature of the aboutness of thought (although he had attended lectures of Franz Brentano, the great theorist of intentionality), still this omission is striking, once called attention to. For the idea of "unconscious" being-represented-to or "unconscious" symbolism (the emphasis here being on the dream contents experienced as something that *happens to* the dreamer and not, as they also in fact are, *creations of* the dreamer) is, like that of the unconscious itself, one that begs for explication. We face, then, not a question of the truth or falsity of Freud's theory of dreams but of its *meaning*—not in the sense of what Freud meant by it but of what kinds of facts in the world could make it true.

Before I attempt to answer this question, let us have a look at a somewhat similar idea in Durkheim's treatment of religion. Like Freud, Durkheim claims that while some states of consciousness have contents that make them ostensibly about certain things or states of affairs, they are "really" about something else; what they symbolize is something unknown to the persons involved, at least in the particular situations. Here is one of Durkheim's formulations of this notion:

> Religion is, first and foremost, a system of ideas by means of which individuals can envisage the society of which they are members, and the relations, obscure yet intimate, which they bear to it. . . . The believer is not deceiving himself when he puts his faith in the existence of a moral potency, on which he is dependent, and to which he owes his better part; this Power exists, it is Society. . . . Doubtless, he is mistaken when he believes that the enhancement of his vital strength is the work of a Being that looks like an animal or a plant. But his error lies only in the literal reading of the symbol by which this Being is presented to his mind, the external aspect under which his imagination conveys it, and does not touch the fact of its existence. Behind these figures and metaphors, however gross or refined they may be, there lies a concrete and living reality.[4]

There are two especially important claims in this passage: first, that religion is the means by which a person may "envisage" society, at least in certain of its characteristics; and second, that despite the nature of the symbol, which, taken literally, treats its object as if it were a conscious being, it in fact symbolizes society itself even if no one is consciously aware of that fact. Presumably, just as, on Freud's theory, dreams have not only always been caused by but have always symbolized repressed wishes even when no one knew or even suspected or imagined otherwise, so, on Durkheim's theory, certain of the symbols of religion have not only always been caused by (though Durkheim doesn't stress this) but have always symbolized society.

There often arises the question of when we should say (because it is a decision about how to use words and not of how the extralinguistic world is) that a person is, for example, perceiving a nonexistent object or instead perceiving an existing object but taking it to have some properties it doesn't have. Such a decision may well be influenced by knowledge of certain causal facts; and if it is clear that the main, relevant cause in a systematic way is a certain object, however misperceived by the person, we may well describe the situation in the latter way. While something like this seems to be going on in both Freud's and Durkheim's the-

---

[4] Emile Durkheim, *The Elementary Forms of the Religious Life*, as quoted in Susanne Langer, *Philosophy in a New Key*, 165–166.

orizing, it is very important to grasp that unless their theories are to be taken as purely causal theories of how people come to have certain dreams and certain religious ideas (making them still important, but very misleadingly stated and much less interesting than they are usually taken to be), each of them must hold also that a person is somehow *represented to* by those dreams and religious ideas. It is of the essence of a symbol, one might well say, that it symbolize; and to symbolize is to stand for, to represent, to be of, to mean, to intend that of which it is the symbol. In particular, Freud and Durkheim each must hold that the person is *presented with* something of which that person is only unconsciously aware, at least by way of having the dream or thinking of a god.

Nor is it adequate or correct to say, as might be suggested on Freud's and Durkheim's behalf, that those contents are symbols only in the sense of being, in other circumstances that are specially related to those of the particular dreamer or believer, the unproblematic symbols of certain wishes and society. This would make the account of dreams and religious beliefs analogous to those accounts of meaning and reference of words in which reference depends, even in the particular case, not on what necessarily goes on in the mind of the particular person who uses the word but instead on the typical or paradigmatic uses of it. Whatever value this notion of "public" meaning may have elsewhere, it is not applicable in the cases at hand: it simply isn't true that dreams (or perceptions generally, of which dreams are a subset) or religious ideas typically or paradigmatically or, for that matter, *ever* do, in the unproblematic sense of what the person is consciously aware of, refer to repressed wishes or to society itself. If they did, then, in the dream case, the wishes wouldn't be repressed but would be fully known to the person who has the dream; and, in the religion case, people would not believe in gods as conscious beings. Furthermore, to the extent that the existence of such symbolism is connected with dream analysis and therapeutic procedures, the public meaning of a symbol insofar as it differs from what is "in" the individual would be wholly irrelevant. It is the symbolism "for" the individual—private meaning, as some would call it—that is of exclusive interest and concern to the analyst.

So we return to the fact that if something is a symbol, it has to be a symbol *for* someone. There is no simple, two-term relation in nature of something's being a symbol of something else, except in the case of natural representation, in which exemplifying a natural sign is just what it is to be aware, in the unproblematic sense (in this context), of something. But that is just the limiting case, so to speak, of representation, while the cases at hand are ones in which their theorists deny that the dreamer or the believer is consciously aware of what, nevertheless, their mental states are said to symbolize.

But because these are not cases of natural representation, at least in the unproblematic sense of conscious awareness, they must somehow involve a "third." That is simply to say that if the dream or religious idea is truly a symbol of something of which the dreamer or believer is not consciously aware, still that dream or idea is a symbol only *to* or *for* that dreamer or believer. But that can only mean that the dreamer or believer stands in some intentional connection to the repressed wish or society itself, if these theories are correct. And so the question becomes, What is this intentional connection and how does it work such that a person is being represented to without conscious awareness of that representation?

In the cases of dreams and religious ideas, it is important to understand that, in the ordinary and here unproblematic sense, the dream is *about* just what it seems to be about and the religious idea is *about* just what it seems to be about. Indeed, as in all cases in which some "real" or "underlying" or "disguised" meaning is to be ascribed to a dream or an idea or a text or anything whatsoever, one must first identity and specify the straightforward conscious meaning, else there is nothing interesting to theorize about. (I would say 'surface meaning', but that expression has been appropriated by some of those who regard the ordinary meaning of what a person says or writes as either nonexistent or as invariably deceptive or ideological or something of that sort, a position from which I wish most emphatically to dissociate myself.) Freud and Durkheim both were aware of this fact and in sense not really aware of it. For a dream that one's house is burning down, whatever it may be said to symbolize, is first and foremost *about* one's house burning down; and the religious idea of a bodiless conscious being who sometimes can be successfully petitioned to change natural events from what they otherwise would have been, whatever it may be said to symbolize, is first and foremost *about* a bodiless conscious being who can change natural events. If the dream is said also to symbolize, say, the repressed wish that one's house be destroyed because of the repressed memory of some shameful sexual act that took place in it, and the religious idea of a god is said also to symbolize the power of society itself, then there must be some *other* intentional state involved in each situation additional to the straightforward one. And again we have the question of what this intentional state is or possibly could be.

Let us pursue this matter with respect to dreams only. But before we can proceed to the only possible answer to the crucial question, we must first ask ourselves just what it is to dream, ontologically speaking. Part of the answer to this question was stated briefly above: dreams form, for the most part, a subset of perceivings. To dream that one's house is burning down is to perceive, probably visually, that one's house is burning down. (As the philosopher always should in matters of the nature of consciousness, I treat dreaming from the first-person point of view.) Thus dreaming is not, ontologically or phenomenologically, a distinct mode of awareness except, as we shall see, to the extent that it also involves the kind of symbolism that Freud claimed for it or any other kind that does not also attach to the perceptions of everyday, waking life. If one's house actually is burning down as one dreams that it is burning down, we may say that the dream is "true" or "veridical" while still probably denying, as the words are used, that one veridically *perceived* that one's house is burning down, just because the usual causal routes, including having one's eyes open, to that kind of perception are absent. It doesn't really matter how we lay the words on the world here provided that we understand clearly that, as experienced or "phenomenologically speaking," to dream is to perceive.

Because the crucial points could easily be restated in any reasonable ontology of mind, no harm will come from employing my own account of states of consciousness, including perceiving, in order to raise a curious issue that Freud never precisely addressed, to my knowledge. The issue can be put roughly by way of asking if it is the burning house of which one is dreaming or the dream of the burning house that is supposed to be the symbol. A burning house is not a dream and a dream is not a burning house, the one being a physical object or occurrence (even if it doesn't exist), the other being a state of consciousness. The problem here derives in part from the frequent ambiguity in the notion of *content*, embracing, as it so often does, both that particular object or event *of* which one is aware and that mental feature *by* which one is aware of some particular object or event. On the account I defended in chapter 4, a perceiving (whether a dream or an ordinary, waking seeing) of one's house burning would be a particular exemplifying the mode property of *being-a-perceiving* and the intentional property (natural sign) of *being-*

of-my-house-burning. The question can now be posed more precisely by asking if it is the burning house or instead its natural sign that is supposed to be the symbol of the repressed wish that one's house be destroyed. If, in waking life, I veridically perceive that my house is burning down, there is no such question to be raised, presumably because I am not myself the relevant part of the cause of my perception—the burning house itself has that role. When I dream that my house is burning down, I am myself, though unknown to me at the time, the most interesting and relevant cause of my own perception. It is this difference in causation that makes the perception in sleep that we call dreaming a situation in which the question of symbolism arises.

Once again we must resist any temptation to say that for the dream content to be a symbol of a certain wish is just for the dream to have been caused by that wish. For in that case, also once more, it is not, in any reasonable sense and not in the sense Freud meant, a symbol at all. Further, the mere causal fact would not have the explanatory power that the fact of genuine symbolization is supposed to have. No, it is required that the dreamer be *presented* with the wish. And this, we are now in a position to grasp, can occur only if something in the dream is a *quasi-natural representation* of the repressed wish, possibly resulting, at some level, in a natural representation of that wish. Obviously it cannot be a purely conventional representation, for that requires the conscious awareness by the person involved of the repressed wish. Nor can it be alone a natural representation, for that would be only an accompanying awareness of the wish even if, in a sense to be explained, it is "unconscious." If the dream itself is a sign of the wish, it can be only a quasi-natural representation.

It should now be clear that the answer to my question above can only be that, strictly speaking, it is the natural sign of the burning house and not the burning house itself that can also play the role of being a quasi-natural sign of the repressed wish. For the natural sign exists but the burning house does not. (And if the burning house does happen to exist, it is playing no causal role in the dream unless it is directly the cause of the dream, in which case Freud too probably would excuse the dream from significant unconscious symbolism.) And in general, when one dreams, the dream and its literal constituents do exist but the objects of one's dreams construed as certain persons and things and events having certain properties do not exist. Dreams are almost always nonveridical with respect to their natural signs but, if Freud is correct, always "veridical" in what they symbolize, at least insofar as it is re-pressed wishes that are symbolized.[5]

But Freud does, of course, also speak of the symbolization of partic-ular kinds of objects and events and to some extent of almost anything whatsoever, that is, of entities that are not repressed wishes. Indeed, in analysis, he looks first at what objects or activities are "symbolized" in order to discover what repressed wish is being "symbolized." Are these different senses of 'symbolize'? I suggest that it is the same sense of the word but that the causal mechanisms are somewhat different in the two kinds of application. On the theory, the symbols of the genitals, most importantly, are "universal" in dreams and do not generally depend on the particular circumstances of the individual person's life except for coming to know the general features of the genitals of both sexes. And genitals are not repressed wishes. But the repressed wishes that are symbolized depend heavily both in their existence and in the ways in which they are symbolized on the particular life circumstances of the individual person. Once again, the literature on the subject, whether or not well-disposed to the theory, seems to take the notion—or notions—of symbolism as unproblematic. But these notions are not unproblem-atic, as is by now quite clear. As for Freud himself on the matter, the fol-lowing passage is instructive in several respects:

Things that are symbolically connected today were probably united in the prehistoric times by conceptual and linguistic identity. The sym-bolic relation seems to be a relic and a mark of former identity. . . . Dreams make use of this symbolism for the disguised representation of their latent thoughts. Incidentally, many of the symbols are habitu-ally or almost habitually employed to express the same thing. Never-theless, the peculiar plasticity of the psychical material [in dreams] must never be forgotten. *Often enough a symbol has to be interpreted in its proper meaning and not symbolically;* while on other occasions a dreamer may derive from his private memories the power to employ as sexual symbols all kinds of things which are not ordinarily employed as such. If a dreamer has a choice open to him between a number of symbols, he will decide in favour of the one which is connected in its subject-

---

[5]   We should not be bothered by the consequence of this reconstruction that one and the same natural sign, considered as a universal, sometimes is and other times is not, a quasi-natural representation. Whether or not a given entity functions as a quasi-natural repre-sentation in a given circumstance may well depend on other aspects of the situation.

matter with the rest of the material of his thoughts—which, that is to say, has individual grounds for its acceptance in addition to the typical ones.[6]

The words I italicized capture the idea, as I put it earlier, of the distinction between the ordinary meaning of the symbol and its possible disguised meaning, even though Freud here reserves the use of 'symbolism' only for the latter function. And one need not take seriously Freud's semi-historical account of the origins of symbolism, whether it be taken as genetic or cultural (or something else), in order to appreciate and consider plausible the general theory of dream symbolism.

For assistance in leading us to an answer to what is fundamentally involved in dream symbolism, and therefore in quasi-natural representation of what the dreamer is at the time not consciously aware of (and ultimately of what I believe to be a similar phenomenon in listening to music), I turn to one of Freud's most devoted admirers and severest critics, Jean-Paul Sartre.

If I am not mistaken, Sartre more or less systematically (but probably not intentionally) overdraws the differences between himself and Freud on the matters of the unconscious and psychoanalysis, in part, I submit, because he overestimates the significance in its consequences of the genuine and radical difference in their views—Freud's scientific determinism and his own radical libertarianism. This overdrawing of differences is involved, I believe, in one of Sartre's basic criticisms of Freud's notion and theory of the unconscious, but it highlights a crucial idea in the entire issue of the possibility of a person's being represented to without conscious awareness of that representation.

Sartre's criticism, set out in the section of his *Being and Nothingness* in which he presents the idea of an *existential psychoanalysis* as an alternative to Freudian psychoanalysis, rests on the so-called "aha" phenomenon, what Sartre calls "the enlightenment of the subject," in which the subject suddenly "recognizes" himself or herself, perhaps as a result of a suggestion by the analyst.[7] On the Freudian view, it would be to recognize that one has a certain, hitherto repressed desire or memory.

---

[6] Sigmund Freud, *On the Interpretation of Dreams*, trans. James Strachey (New York: Avon, 1965), 387–388, my emphasis.

[7] Jean-Paul Sartre, *Being and Nothingness: An Essay on Ontological Phenomenology*, trans. Hazel E. Barnes (New York: Washington Square Press, 1966), 703; *BN* in the text.

On the Sartrean theory, it would be to come to know one's "original project." Sartre's argument is that this phenomenon, in either case, is explainable and, indeed, intelligible only on the assumption that the subject was already, at some level, aware of what is revealed and acknowledged. (*BN*, 703). (Sartre expresses this idea by saying that, prior to the revelation, one is *conscious* of but does not yet have *knowledge* of one's own original project. Thus what one is merely conscious of for Sartre corresponds to what is for Freud in the unconscious, while what one has knowledge of for Sartre corresponds to what for Freud is in the conscious mind—a terminological awkwardness that it is important to see *through*.) It is precisely Sartre's characterization of Freud's notion of the unconscious as a repository of desires and memories of which the conscious mind has no awareness whatsoever that seems to me to be mistaken; but we take his undoubted difference of emphasis as important to suggesting again that *where there is symbolization by a person of something of which that person is not consciously aware, there must also be awareness at some level in the ordinary sense*. Put another way: if the conscious awareness is of X but symbolizes Y, then there must also be some other level of awareness of Y. Or in my language: if some conscious state is a natural representation of X but also a quasi-natural representation of Y, then there must also be a conscious state that is a natural representation of Y. But how can this be, and what exactly does it mean?

We now have need of establishing a less confusing terminology, and we may do that by considering some examples that will also help to clarify the basic idea, as we have so far spoken, of an awareness that is not a conscious awareness.

Consider, then, ordinary perception. Of whatever is in the visual field and of which, therefore, one is at least to some degree perceptually aware, one is usually though not always focusing on some proper part. Typically, too, that on which one is focusing is also that to which one is *attending* in one's perceptual field. But it may be instead the case either (1) that one is attending to something in one's visual field that is not what one is visually focusing on or (2) that one is not attending to much of anything in one's visual field, whether or not one is focusing on anything, but attending instead to something one is hearing or touching or just thinking about. As I emphasized in chapter 4, on the general nature of consciousness, at nearly any moment of one's waking life one is aware, with widely differing levels of attention, of numerous "things":

all or nearly all of one's outer senses are employed; one has various bodily sensations; one is thinking about this and worrying about that; and so on. The fundamental notion here is that of *attention* or, as I have called it in an article in which I suggest possible ontological analyses of the phenomenon, *attending-to*.[8]

Whether or not one is attending to something one is also seeing, there will almost always be some things in one's visual field to which one is attending only very slightly. And indeed, in the limiting case, we may say that one is visually aware of something but is not attending to it at all. Yet another way to express this idea is to say that one is aware of something but does not know and may not remember that one is aware of it. It is thus entirely a mistake to suppose—as philosophers of many stripes have supposed, whether in defense of the idea of consciousness as "private" states or in criticism of that idea—that to be aware of something is to know that one is aware or that to be aware is to be aware that one is aware or the like.

But there is another important distinction to be made here that is relevant to the application of these ideas to dreams and religious ideas and ultimately to music. In the case of someone's being merely visually aware of something, that is, without attending to it at all, it will ordinarily be the case that were that person asked now to attend to that something, he or she would find no obstacle to doing so, perhaps even without any change of focus. Anyone with normal perceptual and neurological apparatus can do this "experiment" alone for that matter, but its outcome hardly needs further verification. On the other hand, what is demanded by Freud's theory of dreams and Durkheim's theory of religious ideas and probably many other theories as well, including Sartre's theory of the original project and my developing theory of musical representation, is that humans have certain kinds of awarenesses that, like the limiting cases of perception, involve no degree of attention but that, unlike those limiting cases, are such that *a person is unable, easily and merely by trying, to attend to what, by the postulated means of consciousness involved, that person is nevertheless aware of.* This idea of awarenesses that do not but also, in an important sense, *cannot* involve attention is fully explicit in Sartre's theory of a typical person's awareness of his or her original project; but while it is also required, if I am not mis-

8   Laird Addis, "Pains and Other Secondary Mental Entities," *Philosophy and Phenomenological Research* 47 (1986), 64–65.

taken, by Freud's and Durkheim's theories, it is never explicitly formulated by them.

It might be asked how it is that a person could be unable to bring
something of which he or she is unconsciously aware into conscious
awareness by some given mode of awareness. This may be asked about
a given theory of such awareness, in which case the answer will depend
on the theory, or it may be asked about a particular case of such unconscious awareness, in which case it will depend on the circumstances
involved. As to the level of theory, Freud's kinds of reasons are well
known; Sartre says that a person is too "close" to the original project
to have conscious awareness—what he calls "knowledge"—of it; in
Durkheim the matter is less clear. In any case, however, the only good
reason for maintaining the existence of such awareness, either as a kind
or in the particular case, is that it is the best explanation of some kind or
instance of a kind of behavior.

Thus we have what may be analytically distinguished as three kinds
or degrees of awareness while fully granting that it is really a matter of
continuum and not of sharply distinguished categories. First, there are
those states of consciousness that do also involve some measure of attention; second, there are those states of consciousness in which there is
no attention but are such that the person could easily attend, by the
same mode of awareness, to the object of that awareness were he or she
pressed to do so; and, third, there are those states of consciousness in
which there is no attention and are such that the person is unable to attend, by the same mode of awareness, to the object of that awareness.[9]
It is important to emphasize that the ability or inability to attend to
something that is involved in these distinctions must be by the same
mode of awareness. For a person who is unable to attend to a repressed
wish even though he or she has through a dream an awareness of it is
aware of and attending to it when the analyst suggests its existence to
that person. Similarly, the Durkheimian believer may certainly attend to

[9] The reader may usefully be reminded that, as I have been using the words, unconscious awareness—shortly to be further divided into inattentive awareness and nonattentive awareness—is a subset of the set of states of consciousness. This terminological
incongruity will cause no difficulty if it is kept in mind that, as I am using the words, any
degree of awareness is a state of consciousness. Freud's idea of the unconscious is best understood not as some kind of awareness but as a set of *dispositions* to have certain kinds of
awarenesses and to behave in certain ways. For further analysis of Freud's notions of unconscious belief and unconscious memory, see Laird Addis, "Dispositional Mental States:
Chomsky and Freud," *Zeitschrift für Allgemeine Wissenschaftstheorie* 19 (1988).

society itself through some other modes of consciousness than that of having religious ideas. The crucial idea here is that of a level and a mode of awareness that, while presenting something to a person, is such that one cannot, by that same mode of awareness, attend to what is being presented to one.

As for terminology, let us label these three levels of awareness in the order just described as: *attentive awareness, inattentive awareness*, and *nonattentive awareness*. And before we apply some of these ideas to music and the emotions, let us apply them very briefly to Freud's theory of symbolism in dreams with the idea that they would apply, *mutatis mutandis*, to Durkheim's theory of symbolism in religion.

A person (visually) dreams that his house is burning down. The dream is said to be symbolic of that person's repressed wish that his house be destroyed because of the repressed memory of a shameful sexual episode that took place in it. The dream, as a perception of the burning house, is an attentive awareness of the house. The very same awareness, as a quasi-natural sign ("symbol") of the wish, is a nonattentive awareness of the wish producing in the dreamer some kind of natural representation of the wish which is also a nonattentive awareness. Why, one may well ask, should we suppose that there is both a quasi-natural and a natural representation of the wish? The answer to that question will become clear if we now turn to the case of music.

8

Music and Awareness

Our excursus into Freud's theory of symbolism in dreams and, to a much lesser extent, Durkheim's theory of symbolism in religion was intended to help us understand, and possibly make more plausible to us, a theory according to which music may symbolize the emotions to a listener without the listener's conscious awareness. But we are faced immediately with a fundamental difference between dreams and religious ideas as symbols on the one hand and music as symbol on the other. That difference is the fact that dreams and religious ideas are themselves conscious states with their own ordinary intentional objects (the burning house, the bodiless being who responds to petitions) while a piece of music is not a conscious state of any kind. A piece of music is not a mental thing at all, not a part of any mind but only the product of a mind and such that, once brought into existence, it enjoys independence from its creator.

Thus in the case of music it is not a matter of having an ordinary meaning as well as a disguised meaning.[1] Nor therefore does one pro-

---

[1] Peter Kivy draws a similar, but importantly different, distinction *within* artworks. He argues that because some paintings, for example, have deeper meanings to be derived from what they quite obviously depict, it is doubtful that music has any deeper or hidden meaning at all just because it has no obvious surface meaning. See *Philosophies of Art*, the chapter called "The Liberation of Music." I see the matter of meaning in artworks (as in language and dreams and possibly religion) as more a matter of a continuum in the sense that within a given medium there is no sharp distinction between surface meaning and deeper meaning and also in the sense that the various media of the arts as well as

ceed to its disguised meaning (as I am willing to call what, on the new theory, music does have) by way of first specifying its ordinary meaning. One can of course describe the music in its acoustical and formal properties, but that is not, except by obscurantist stipulation, either *the* or *a* meaning of the music, especially if we regard what is meant as always something distinct from the entity that means it: the meaning relation is most usefully conceived always as one that presupposes the nonidentity of its terms, contrary to the fashionable but opaque postmodernist concern with "self-reference" and the equally abstruse idea that texts are only about texts.

In this respect, then, music is more like language than dreams and religious ideas. For language also, at least as sound and inscription, is not something mental even though its intentionality is more closely tied, analytically, to that of the literal intentionality of consciousness than is the intentionality, if there be such, of music—at least on the new theory. This is just another way of saying that language as sound and inscription consists of conventional signs, but that music, on the new theory, consists of quasi-natural signs, giving the latter greater independence from the literal intentionality of consciousness.

Music, to repeat, is not anything mental. It is not conscious nor ontologically dependent on anything that is conscious. As such, and like everything that is not a state of consciousness, it does not possess literal intentionality in the sense of being, in and of itself, *about* anything. The aboutness or intentionality of anything that is not a state of consciousness—from language to music and other artworks, from graphs and maps and charts to the workings of computers, from gestures and facial expressions to rituals and games—depends ultimately on, by deriving in some manner from, the intrinsic and literal intentionality of consciousness. When there was no consciousness in the universe, as in its first several billion years, there was, whatever resemblances and isomorphisms existed, no *aboutness* whatsoever.

With these reminders, we may proceed finally to the ontological analysis of what goes on in listening to a piece of music with respect to its

---

language, dreams, and so on may themselves form something of an ordered set with respect to the proportion of each kind of meaning that is typical in an instance of it. Thus music may be one end of this "continuum" in having almost no surface meaning and a lot of deeper meaning. But I agree that where there is surface meaning, it is the main key to the deeper meaning.

(semi-derived) intentionality, making use of the terminology introduced toward the end of the immediately preceding chapter. There will be three relevant cases to consider in which, by assumption, the music is sad: the case in which the listener is consciously in mind of sadness, the case in which the listener is not consciously in mind of sadness but acquires the disposition to describe the music as sad, and the case in which the listener, while familiar with the style of the music, neither is put in mind of sadness nor acquires the disposition to describe the music as sad. (If the listener is also caused to *feel* sad, as contrasted with merely being put in mind of sadness, so be it; I am by now simply assuming the falsity of any theory that would regard the occurrence of such a feeling as analytically relevant to understanding the sadness of the music.)

Let us begin with what in a sense is, for the new theory, the easiest case: that of the listener who is not particularly conscious of sadness while listening to the music but who comes to be strongly disposed to describe the music as sad as a result of listening to it. In this case, we shall say that the listener has an *attentive awareness of the music* itself and a *nonattentive awareness of sadness* itself, the latter due to the quasi-natural representation of sadness by the music to the listener. The music presents sadness to the listener who is familiar with the musical style, somewhat as the word *sadness* presents sadness to a person who knows the English language. But *somewhat* as a person might hear and understand a conversation without significant attentive awareness, so the listener is presented with sadness without attentive awareness. And the listener's acquisition of the disposition to describe the music as sad is best explained by just that supposition.

Here again there is an important disanalogy with Freud's theory of symbolism in dreams. The dreamer, after all, does *not* acquire the disposition to describe himself or herself as having the wish of which he or she is said to be unconsciously aware. And the theory contains—all too smoothly, some would say—an explanation of why that is so. But that is only the special nature of Freud's theory. And, as on my theory, according to which the listener does acquire the disposition to describe the music in the language of what has been presented by the music through unconscious awareness, it is some aspect of *behavior*, even if not, in the Freudian case, the behavior of describing something in the language of what one has been unconsciously aware, that is involved.

Consider now the first case, in which the listener *is* in mind of sadness. Here again we have an *attentive awareness of the music* and, by assumption, also an *attentive awareness of sadness*, the latter with possibly a lesser degree of attention. The listener is hearing the music and is in mind of sadness. But I want to insist that, by another mode of awareness, the listener is also being presented with sadness by the music and that there is, accordingly, also a *nonattentive awareness of sadness* taking place. There is nothing paradoxical or even unfamiliar in the idea of multiple, simultaneous modes of awareness of the same thing, the simplest and clearest kind of case probably being that of seeing and touching the same object at the same time. But we commonly also, for example, see and think about the same object at the same time, and I am suggesting that something like this sometimes takes place in listening to music in which the nonattentive awareness of sadness corresponds to the seeing while the attentive awareness of sadness just *is* the thinking about. And if we take notice of studies of so-called unconscious seeing (sometimes called "blindsight") in stroke victims and others and other similar phenomena that could be invoked as examples of nonattentive awareness, we can construct an even tighter analogy. For the person who is, by perception, nonattentively aware of something is, at the same time, quite able, in attentive awareness, to think about what he or she is seeing but is unable to attend to through seeing.

The third case—that of the listener who, while familiar with the musical style of the sad music, is neither in mind of sadness nor disposed to describe the music as sad—is clearly the most complicated and, accordingly, the most difficult for the new theory. Here again there is, by assumption, an attentive awareness of the music itself. If there is not attentive awareness of the music, there is not really anything to be accounted for and we need not consider that as a separate case, even though a person certainly can have at least an inattentive awareness of music, as we often do in fact, and possibly also a nonattentive awareness, as possibly in certain kinds of stroke victims and others with brain damage. So we assume attentive awareness of the music in the case to be examined.

Is there, then, on my account, also nonattentive awareness of sadness in this case, even though the relevant disposition is not acquired? Here one might want more details of the uncontroversial part of the description of the situation, but the general answer to the question is sometimes yes and sometimes no. For if the listener is not disposed later to describe the music as sad but also not disposed to describe it in any other way (putting aside all matters of shyness, difficulty in speaking, inebriation, general mendacity, and so on), we may say simply that such nonattentive awareness either failed to take place or that, having taken place, other factors blocked the acquisition of the disposition. Here again we can imagine an analogy of hearing a conversation in a language one understands but failing to remember, even a short time later, what the topic was or what was said about it.

But how about the person who not only is not disposed to describe the music as sad but who has acquired the disposition to describe it as joyful? While such an extreme difference in acquired disposition on the parts of listeners who, by assumption, are familiar with the style of the music is not very common, less extreme differences in the characterization of a particular piece or passage of music by knowledgeable listeners are very common. And some account of this phenomenon is surely called for from anyone who maintains that the emotional qualities of music are inherent in the music itself even if only by way of what the music represents.

We are not concerned here with differences in the *evaluation* of a piece of music—as worthy or not worthy, beautiful or not beautiful, sublime or not sublime—for while these characterizations are not entirely unrelated to those involving the predications of mood and emotion, the predicates of *aesthetic value* may be regarded, like those of moral value, as only reflecting a person's attitudes toward the music (or, in the moral case, toward the action or person) and not as picking out any objective properties of the music.[2] What a particular person "likes" or finds "beautiful" and what persons and actions deems "virtuous" or "desirable" is a matter of temperament and training and, in some measure, reflection of a certain kind, and not of anything directly discovered in nature itself. I am suggesting, however—though always agreeing and even insisting that some learning is involved—that the sadness of the music is objectively there in the music in the sense that

[2] This "subjectivism" or "relativism" on my part in aesthetic and moral matters is not intended as any part of an account of what people may "mean" when they make aesthetic or moral utterances. Meaning analysis, characteristic of a certain school of analytic philosophy, is of little philosophical and no ontological significance at all except to help us identify the precise object of investigation. And, probably needless to say, the advocate of such a "subjectivism" need not deny that the objective properties of artworks, persons, and actions and the perception and knowledge of those properties are important parts of the causal basis for the use of the predicates of aesthetics and ethics. But saying that some of those objective properties are what is "really" meant by those predicates is either simply false as a matter of anthropological fact or else a trivial decision about how the speaker proposes to use certain words.

the connection of that music to sadness by way of human nature is a matter of certain laws of nature connecting certain properties of the music to sadness. But the truth or falsity of my theory about music does not in any way depend on my "subjectivism" in aesthetics and ethics as just characterized.

So our problem of accounting for the difference in acquired dispositions remains to be solved.

One way to describe what may go on in the hearing of music, on the new theory, is to say that the listener, while familiar with the style, has nevertheless *misunderstood* the music. Misunderstanding presupposes the possibility of understanding. Just as person who knows a given language may sometimes misunderstand a conversation in that language, so a person may, as it were, hear a piece of music with a wrong presupposition or a failure to appreciate the sense of an extension of the style (as, for example, those even knowledgeable listeners who couldn't make sense of Wagner's music because they didn't realize that it was a development *within* the style they already knew) or the failure to realize something as the musical equivalent of metaphor or irony in language. The sense in which, in such cases, one actually has been presented with the emotion or mood that the music represents but failed to take on the requisite disposition is not easy to specify. But the problem of so specifying, or of imagining the very idea of it, will be seen to be less of an objection to the new theory if one also sees that the same problem arises with respect to language where there is no controversy about its possession, even if derivatively, of semantic properties.

Thus, as in language, a person may be not only not presented, or not fully presented, with what the music actually represents but indeed put in mind of a different emotion or caused to acquire a different disposition from the state of mind or disposition appropriate to the represented emotion. People have to come to *learn*—by appreciating the musical style, by knowing the context of a passage or even an entire movement of a piece of music, by grasping a new "dialect" of the style they already know, by listening carefully and attentively in memory of what has gone before—what a given piece of music "means" and to allow the full force of what the music represents actually to be presented to them, even if only nonattentively. This all fits well with the fact that, again as with language, a younger person can come to understand and appreciate a "second" or "third" musical style more easily than can an older person. One is reminded in this connection of Picasso's famous reply to the objection that his painting of Gertrude Stein didn't look like her: "Never mind, it will!" While the remark itself admits of several interpretations and can be used to buttress a number of salient points about representation in the arts (Picasso's own meaning being not entirely irrelevant, of course), the point I draw from it is that sometimes one has to learn what is being presented to one; or, to put it another way, one has to learn how to prepare oneself to allow the presentation fully to take place. Most people are unwilling even to try in altogether too many cases; but for those who are so willing, the rewards are often beyond what, for them, is all conceivable expectation.

Another aspect of this matter, to which I have alluded once or twice, deserves elaboration here. I have granted and even insisted that, while the quasi-natural representation of the emotions by music, deriving from the ontological affinity of consciousness and sound, is the most important connection of music to the emotions in the explanation of its power for us and of the relevant anthropological and phenomenological data, there are other connections as well that link music to the emotions in nontrivial ways. (Everything is "connected" to everything else in some way or other.) I am especially agreeable to Kivy's thesis that some properties of music actually *resemble* some of the facial and other behavioral expressions of the emotions, as well as to Langer's supposition that some properties of music also *resemble* some of the physiological aspects of the emotions, at least in some measure. And it *may* be too that there is a direct causal link, independent of one's being presented by the emotions, that occasionally arouses or puts the listener in mind of the emotions that the music represents, although I doubt it. Music unquestionably does stir the emotions, but the emotion stirred is rarely the emotion that the music represents, a point to which I shall return in the final chapter.

The new theory, therefore, places no restrictions on the ways in which, by music, the emotions are aroused, brought to mind, actually and potentially described or referred to, and otherwise connected to music. It insists only that what underlies all of these several connections is the basic ontological tie between consciousness and sound and the quasi-natural representation of certain states of consciousness by sound and especially by music (without much worry therefore just what actual and possible subsets of sounds are music.)

I mention these other connections of the emotions to music just because, as may already be obvious, they will sometimes complicate and oddly affect the actual effects on a listener to music or a particular piece of music. And just as contradictory or confused things can be said and written down in various ways, so confused and "contradictory" music can be composed. Thus a generally sad piece of music may also have properties that resemble the behavioral expression of other, "opposite" emotions or moods, an unskillful composer perhaps failing to make a certain section as long as it should be or overdoing the dynamics or using too thin an orchestration.

And so, while the new theory is intended in large part to explain the power and importance of music in human affairs, it is at least consistent with the fact of the varieties of effects that a given piece of music may have on a knowledgeable set of listeners, as we have seen. At the same time, if I am correct, the fact of this variety does not diminish the plausibility of the theory in explaining that power any more than the fact of, say, the varying effects of vaccines affects the plausibility of the germ theory of certain diseases. When, after all, does one ever have truly necessary and sufficient conditions in matters causal?

I have stated that the main defense of the theory that, by virtue of the isomorphism between consciousness and sound and of human nature, music is a quasi-natural representation of certain states of consciousness is (1) that it is internally consistent and also consistent with all the relevant facts concerning people and music, and (2) that it is the *best explanation* of those facts concerning people and music. Chapter 7 and the preceding pages of this one have been intended to establish the first of these beyond reasonable doubt without claiming formal demonstration, which is impossible by the nature of the case. In the appendix, in which I go to the literature for criticisms of any theory of the type of the new theory and attempt brief replies to them, I discuss some further issues of consistency and coherence. But assuming that the new theory does possess the characteristics that make it *possibly true*, I want here to defend the claim of best explanation.

Best explanations are, to be sure, always relative both to the set of explanations of the same phenomena (*pace* Thomas Kuhn) that have actually been conceived and publicized and to the arguments and evidence for and against each of those theories. As to the set to be considered, it consists of exactly the members of those five kinds of theories I set out in the first chapter; and while in most cases I will have little to add by

way of new arguments against them—especially the causal theories—
it will be appropriate and useful to consider each kind separately in order to strengthen my claim that the new theory is the best theory of the
most important connection of music to the emotions. At the same time,
such discussion will make clearer the very meaning and import of the
new theory.

The composer-causal theory of emotion in music is, I believe, absurd
on its face, for it tells us that to know the emotional qualities of a given
piece of music is really to know something of the biography, and the
"inner" biography at that, of the composer of the music. Whatever interest such facts may have (to whatever extent they may be available),
they fail *altogether* to explain either the power music has on human beings or the specific facts about human feelings of, thoughts of, and dispositions to ascribe to the music certain emotions and other conscious
states. It would be similar to supposing that one could explain the effect
of consuming aspirin on human physiology and sensation by knowing
the motives or feelings of its manufacturers. Furthermore, the theory
presupposes what is either factually false or unknowable—that there is
some significant similarity of feelings and intentions and mental procedures among most or all composers in their activity of composing. The
fact is that there is no such similarity, not even always in the same composer at different times. Anyone who has composed music or, for that
matter, engaged in any systematic creative work, whether in the arts or
in science or in the humanities or elsewhere, knows the presupposition
to be false from his or her own experience.

A listener-causal theory of emotion in music is at least aimed at
explaining what goes on in listening to music—directly, as it were.
Whether in the form of the arousal theory in which it is sadness itself
that is produced in the listener or the somewhat more plausible form in
which it is the thought of sadness that is produced, the music as perceived is irrelevant in the sense that its inherent, perceivable qualities
don't matter to the account: music is like a sadness pill that one could
take, causing either sadness or the thought of sadness, and how it
achieves its effect is irrelevant to the theory that to be a sad piece of music is just to have that power.

Appreciating that the logical form of the theory is the same as the pill-
taking account enables us to see its weakness. For while it may allow
that, in fact, it is the perceptions of certain features of the music that
produce the effects in the listener that are to be explained, it must also

allow, insofar as it is a purely causal account of the analytic kind of what it is for a piece of music to be sad, that any kind of music whatsoever *might have*, or *might have had*, the typical effect of causing sadness or the thought of sadness in the listener. And while of course that is true in some sense in any case, at least if one also holds that it is a fully contingent matter what causes what, this suggestion of the contingency of causation might seem to be the basis of an objection to the new theory as well.

We are faced here with a difficult and curious issue that only barely can be alluded to and that has to do, generally, with questions of contingency and necessity with respect to states of consciousness and their objects in particular and, by extension, to philosophical theories themselves. The question is difficult even to state clearly but it has to do with whether or not there could be a systematic displacement between the natures of our awarenesses and their effects, that is, whether or not it is even intelligible to suppose that, for example, what are awarenesses, even attentive awarenesses, of cows could result in the disposition to describe what has been seen as carrots. It may help in this connection to mention a similar, but much more widely discussed, issue in action theory, which may be put as a question. If the connection between having a reason for an action and the action itself is contingent, then couldn't any reason go, even systematically, with any action?

The issue has not to do with the mere fact that one's perception was caused by a cow or the mere fact that one might use the word *carrot* to describe what one took to be a cow, but instead with the possibility that while one was aware of a cow *as* a cow, one acquired as result of the perception a disposition to describe what one saw as what we now call a carrot. Wondering whether or not this is possible and also wondering about its relevance to the evaluation of the listener-causal theory of emotion in music is also to wonder about the logical status of any of the theories of emotion in music. I would say that, in general, the task of philosophy, at least as ontology, is to describe certain features of reality—features that are either or both beyond the capacity of empirical science to describe (such as, and probably only, the "inner" life) or are to be characterized in a way that is quite different from the descriptions of empirical science. I do not, therefore, share the worries of a certain branch of analytic philosophy—the school of so-called conceptual analysis—whether or not philosophical theories are "necessary" or "contingent," partly because I regard what are called "conceptual analyses" as based on the illusion that some significant discovery can be made, whereas what is actually going on is either linguistic anthropology or else stipulation of meaning.

With these probably altogether too succinct remarks (but this is not a treatise on method in philosophy), let us return to the evaluation of the listener-causal theory. This theory is not, to my mind, to be rejected because it is *merely* a causal theory and so not "necessary" as the conceptual analysts might wish to demand. I reject it on the phenomenological ground that in the crucial respect sad music simply is not like a sadness pill: it *is* in virtue of the qualities of the music I perceive and *as* perceived that it puts me in mind of sadness (if it does) and that I acquire the disposition to describe the music as sad (if I do). One would never be tempted to describe a pill as sad because of its power to make a person sad or be in mind of sadness, even if one had to perceive the pill as well as ingest it for it to produce its effect. And even if we did come, with such knowledge, to describe the pill itself as sad, would we not still know full well that there is some important difference of kind between what makes the pill sad and what makes music sad? There thus remains the question of what the connection is between the perceived (whether or not attentively) properties of music and the emotions themselves such that the perception of those properties has the effect it does on listeners.

The pure-inherence theory is, as far as I can tell, Kivy's own innovation. As I suggested earlier, I am not convinced that it is an intelligible theory in the sense of being one truly distinct from either a causal theory or a representative theory. It would seem that there is no "space" between theories that hold that music simply causes the relevant effects in listeners due to some basic laws of nature and theories that maintain that the music as perceived somehow manages to represent the emotions to listeners. Indeed, Kivy's main argument for his theory appears to be that neither causal nor representative theories can do the job (keeping in mind, as he himself notes, that he holds or held a kind of representative theory with respect to some but not all cases of emotion in music). One should not be opposed in principle to arguments of this kind, and my own argument itself is in some measure of this kind as well—that all the competitors to the favored theory are inadequate. But just as Kivy argues that representative theories require what he calls "unconscious representation" and so are ultimately incoherent, so I claim that his theory only appears to be a possible account of the matter.[3] His idea of an "expressive property" that is a property of the music itself but that has no representative character is not quite like the idea of the property of *being-neither-red-nor-not-red*, but it's something like that. Kivy has made one distinction too many.

In defense of his theory Kivy does not seem to make any positive argument or characterization of expressive properties beyond his repeated insistence that music has such properties, that they are musical properties, and that composers deliberately put such properties in their music. The closest thing to an argument for his view, which comes by way of an argument against any representative theory, appears in this passage:

> So anyone who wishes to argue that because "sad" has a reference not only to music but, far more basically, to conscious human states, it follows that sad music must be about sadness, will have to argue as well that because "tranquil" and "quiet" and "turbulent" have reference not only to music but, far more basically, to natural phenomena and human behavior, it follows that tranquil and quiet and turbulent music must be about those things: about tranquil days, quiet nights, turbulent lives. But surely that is absurd. (*MA*, 194)

There are several issues here. The first is whether or not some or all of the properties of *being-tranquil, being-quiet,* and *being-turbulent* are literal properties of the music itself in the sense that *being-sad* clearly is not just because in the literal sense it can be a property only of a conscious being. Those properties that are literal properties of the music itself may then be distinguished from *being-sad* in the relevant way that leaves open the problem of the sadness of the music. Those that are not such literal properties may yet raise the next question: whether or not they may not also represent emotions or other kinds of conscious states instead of days, nights, and lives. In the ontological affinity of consciousness and sound, I have located a special reason for maintaining that if music represents

[3]   It should be well noted that Kivy's argument about "unconscious representation" in music is concerned solely with its alleged capacity to explain our pleasure in music and not with any disposition to apply the predicates of emotion. See *Music Alone*, 58–62; *MA* in the text. I have not argued, and do not argue, about the sources of pleasure in music anywhere in this book (or else everywhere!) except very briefly in the final chapter. And Kivy is clear that he is not denying the very possibility of unconscious perceptions in music or elsewhere, only their power to explain pleasure in music.

anything, it is states and features of consciousness. I find no absurdity in supposing that to whatever extent, depending on the context, the applications of the predicates in question are not intended as literal characterizations of the music itself, what are picked out are features of the music that represent states or features of consciousness.

Thus, despite his many interesting observations about the musical nature of expressive properties and their appearance or absence in this or that piece of music, I submit that Kivy's theory fails to account for the relevant anthropological and phenomenological facts—why we apply the predicates of emotion and mood to music. It is just not enough to say, if I may somewhat caricature his argument for the sake of the point: "Those properties are just there! See how the composer did it? We call them *expressive* properties and they are really in the music itself. And don't worry about how they connect with the emotions themselves; that will only lead you to absurd and unintelligible ideas of representation." I conclude that the pure-inherence theory of emotion in music is simply an incomplete and therefore an inadequate theory: it fails to have any account of why some musical properties should also be expressive properties.

That leaves, in my judgment, only representative theories as plausible candidates for the best explanation of the relevant facts. Possibly representative theories could take some forms that have not yet been conceived; and my theory, resting as it does, and as no previous theory has, on the ontological affinity of consciousness and sound, I have offered as a "new" theory. But it is a form of an intentionality-inherence theory, as I have used the words, in contrast to a resemblance-inherence theory, the distinction between the two kinds resting on the possibly dubious distinction between resemblance and isomorphism on the one hand and, on the other, between a notion of representation that would locate the distinction between symbol and symbolized in that between artifact (music) and nature (the emotions) and one that would find it in the ontological affinity of consciousness and sound and quasi-natural representation. Which is the better kind of theory and why?

Resemblance theories, if they are not also isomorphism theories, fall short, I submit, first because in most cases the required resemblance between properties of the music and the outward expression of emotion is simply absent or, at best, present in such a stretched way as to make the theory either artificial or trivial. Davies' theory, that "the expressiveness of music depends mainly on a resemblance we perceive between the

dynamic character of music and human movement, gait, bearing, or car-
riage" seems to me to be one of this sort.[4] Furthermore, while no doubt
sometimes there are such resemblances as the theory calls attention to,
it requires a kind of prior knowledge of those outward expressions that
seems at least sometimes to be missing, even when the listener regards
the music in its emotional properties. And because the connection
between the emotions themselves (or the emotions as felt) and their
outward expression is itself purely contingent and lawful given an organism of a certain kind, there is no intrinsic connection of any kind between music and the emotions themselves, on the theory. The resemblance theory, here understood as involving resemblance to expression
of the emotions and not the emotions themselves, thus comprises an altogether weak and superficial notion of representation.

The best theory, then, in accounting for the connections between music and the emotions is the new theory: it makes the emotions and other
states of consciousness themselves the objects that are represented, it
provides a deep ontological ground for the idea that music is a representation of the quasi-natural kind of states of consciousness to human
beings, and it explains how this representation can take place even in
the absence of its conscious recognition by musical listeners.

Finally, to return to the point from which we began this investigation,
the new theory explains why human like music. More precisely, taking
for granted something that, in another context, might itself call for
explanation, it identifies listening to music as one of those many kinds
of circumstances in which emotion and mood are *presented* to us and
which thereby *affect* our emotions. One can hardly begin to enumerate
the many ways—from ritual and religion to television shows in which
people bare their innermost (if usually still shallow) feelings—that
somehow involve the presentation of emotion. Music allows such presentation to take place in relative independence of particular persons;
indeed, if I am correct, we are sometimes presented with mood and
emotion that no one has ever felt while at other times, at least in my experience, it seems that the music perfectly expresses a feeling that I have
had but could not name. From my own experience, I think again of
Arnold Schoenberg's *Five Orchestral Pieces* as presenting both hitherto
unfelt and still unnamed emotion and mood.

[4] Stephen Davies, *Musical Meaning and Expression* (Ithaca: Cornell University Press,
1994), 229.

Music then *affects* the emotions by *presenting* us with emotions; and it is not surprising that the effect of music on us is often not dissimilar to situations in which we observe strong emotion in other humans. Of course, language can present the emotions too, sometimes with powerful effect. But music does it ever so much more easily, so to speak, just because, as the new theory maintains, first, it can present ranges and subtleties of feeling that language cannot and, second, that it is a quasi-natural and not just a conventional representation of feelings.

I turn in my final chapter to some reflections on the emotion *felt* in listening to music.

9

Music as Stirring

S everal times, usually in the context of disputing the listener-causal theory of emotion in music, I have made a distinction between emotion *in* music and emotion *from* music. The key idea is that the emotions we *feel* in listening to music are not ordinarily those emotions we hear in, or acquire the disposition to ascribe to, the music. Sad music does not typically make a person feel sad, although the conventions of concertgoing require a more somber demeanor while listening to such music than in listening to marches. Having made this distinction (and intending to provide no further systematic argument against the listener-causal account of emotion in music), I propose to end this essay with some reflections on emotion *from* music. For, assuming the falsity of the listener-causal theory, there does remain the question of the connection of music as heard to emotion as felt, even if the answer may be that there is no general connection across the species or even across a relevantly specified subset of it members, such as regular listeners to European-American art music.

Peter Kivy seems to hold some such heterogeneous account of emotion from music in his *Sound Sentiment* when, in rejecting what he calls the "arousal" theory of emotion *in* music, he maintains that

If music, then, arouses the full-blooded emotions—fear, anger, sadness, and the like—and I believe it can and sometimes does, it arouses them in something like the good old-fashioned way. . . : through the association of ideas. . . . And the association of ideas . . . is irretrievably private and idiosyncratic—not the publicly negotiable medium we require for an account of the expressiveness of music that would satisfy the contemporary musician and "scientific" musicologist. (*SS*, 32)

But Kivy refers in this passage only to what he here calls the "full-blooded" emotions and elsewhere the "non-musical" emotions, suggesting as have many others that there might be an emotion that is peculiar to musical experience and that is not one of the ordinary "full-blooded" emotions, the emotion that Johann Hiller two centuries ago characterized as "unknown [i.e., unnamed] by us, but it excites pleasure in us, and that suffices."[1] But in fact Kivy rejects the idea of such an emotion in any nontrivial sense:

It is, of course, a harmless truism that music "arouses" pleasure, since to say this is to say nothing more surprising or controversial than that we—some of us, anyway—enjoy music. But that music arouses in us some unique musical emotion—a special case of the well-known theory that art arouses unique "aesthetic emotions"—is, it appears to me, an untenable view, long since given up by most philosophers of art for reasons I think it would be pointless and boring to rehash here yet again. (It will suffice, I think, to put it to the reader whether, in his or her experience, the same emotion or feeling is always felt in hearing music, or in hearing the same music at different times, or even throughout the entire hearing of one piece of music at one given time.) (SS, 98)

I put it to the reader that, while one should agree that there is no aesthetically interesting or regular connection of the emotions that are felt in listening to music to the emotions that are expressed by the music (or any other of its properties), there is, in fact, a distinctive emotion that music arouses (in some people anyway) that is not just the admittedly trivial circumstance that people enjoy listening to music, although it is connected with that circumstance. Further, I submit (rejecting without argument the largely Wittgensteinian epistemological concerns that have led many contemporary philosophers to Kivy's kind of disregard for the theory) that most listeners to music can find this emotion or

[1] Johann Hiller, "Abhandlung von der Nachahmung der Natur in der Musik," as quoted in Peter Kivy, *Sound Sentiment*, 98.

feeling within themselves, if they are properly instructed on what to look for and how to find it. Kivy's way is not the proper way, for the thesis that there is a distinctive emotion aroused by listening to music requires neither (1) that it be felt in listening to music on every occasion; nor (2) that if ever it is felt in listening to a given piece of music, it must be felt every time one hears that piece of music; nor, least of all, (3) that it be felt at every moment in listening to a piece of music.

A well-known composer reported that after hearing Richard Wagner's *Parsifal* for the first time he cried for two weeks. Although this cannot be literally true, I believe I know exactly the feeling that caused this extreme and extended response to the music. And we may note immediately that the intelligibility of the thesis that this feeling is reasonably identified as an "unique aesthetic emotion" does not require that it occur in connection with hearing just any piece of music or that it occur, if at all, every time one hears the same music or that it persist throughout the hearing of a given piece of music. Indeed, it may occur only, or most evidently or strongly, *after* hearing the music, just as other emotions often occur only, or most strongly, after the events that precipitate them. Feelings of grief, anger, nostalgia, and many more quite typically persist and even intensify long after the events that, in the relevant sense, are their causes have ceased to exist. So we must reject the test that Kivy puts to the reader-cum-listener as to whether or not he or she has such feelings.

One might say, if one were prone to speculative theories of a certain type, that just as, for Schopenhauer, music represents the will itself, what is aroused by music is *emotion itself*. I know I am not alone—in fact, I suspect that nearly the opposite is the case—in being able to report that, *sometimes*, when all of the ordinary emotions that have been aroused or enhanced or diminished by listening to a piece of music have been identified, there remains something else for which the first word that may come to mind is 'stirring', the second probably 'excitement' but in the original or earlier sense of being stirred. Yet it is not just the momentary excitement of listening to *The Stars and Stripes Forever* that I am referring to, a kind that is likely to last little beyond the hearing, but something that goes "deeper" and is likely to be more durable. I remember clearly the occasion on which I felt this "emotion," if that really is the right word, most strongly (although listening to *Parsifal* can still approximate it in me) when, as a fifteen-year-old out with my parents' car, I turned on the radio and heard for the first time Igor Stravinsky's *Le Sacre du Printemps*. It took me several days to calm down; and even now, after dozens of hearings, the feeling is still aroused.[2]

Kivy and other critics of the theory of "aesthetic emotion" surely know of such experiences and such feelings. And indeed Kivy in his *Music Alone* argues at great length and persuasively about the existence and the nature of the emotion that music arouses, his main motive apparently being to show that one can deny the arousal account (what I call the listener-causal account) of emotion in music without in the least denying the power of music to arouse emotion. What then is the argument, between Kivy and me (or Kivy and Kivy) about—what to *call* this emotion, whether or not it is *always* there in listening to music, whether or not it is *unique* to music listening or only to the appreciation of artworks in general? Much of this debate about "aesthetic emotion" does seem to me to have little significance, but there is one issue concerning it upon which Kivy is particularly insistent and which seems to me worthy of further discussion.

In his *Music Alone*, Kivy severely attacks a critic of his, Peter Mew, who argues that the emotion aroused specifically by music is an objectless emotion (*MA*, 166–169). Worrying at some length about what the mechanism might be by which music would arouse such an emotion, Kivy claims that only someone already convinced of the conclusion would respond favorably to Mew's assertion that reflection on one's own musical experiences will "clinch the matter."[3] Mew's view, unfortunately, is that the objectless emotion aroused by music is also the emotion that the music expresses, and that aspect of his view has been rejected many times over by both Kivy and me.

At the same time, I want to suggest, *contra* Kivy, that there is an objectless emotion that is uniquely aroused by music. It is not, as has been emphatically insisted, the emotion in the music; it is the "stirring," the being moved that Kivy himself unequivocally acknowledges and that

---

[2] The "emotion" is not entirely pleasant. Perhaps it is only an accident of evolution that in humans the outward facial expression of this emotion, when uninhibited, can be very similar to that of pain and of orgasm. Others must have noted this three-term similarity, but I know of no systematic investigation, empirical or otherwise, into it.

[3] Peter Mew, "The Expression of Emotion in Music," *British Journal of Aesthetics* 25 (1985), 35.

he ascribes to recognition of the "beauty" of the music. As to its special character, here is what he says in *Sound Sentiment:*

> I am saying there is a "special" musical emotion, but only in the most benign, nominalistic sense. When I am moved by the beauty of music, I am experiencing "a" or "the" musical emotion, simply in virtue of my having been moved by the beauty of *music*, rather than by the beauty of something else. I am saying nothing more "metaphysical" than I would be if I said there is a special botanical emotion, namely, the emotion I get when I am moved by the beauty of a plant or flower. (*SS*, 231)

I have no interest in challenging the thesis that what makes the music emotion special is merely that it is caused by listening to music. But I do wish to affirm that it is an objectless emotion and, in the closing section of this essay, to argue that unless beauty be regarded as *whatever it is* in music that arouses this emotion, the idea that it *is* the beauty of music that moves us is far too narrow a conception of the power and the nature of music.

Kivy's worry about the mechanism whereby music might cause an objectless emotion seems to be quite groundless and not, in any case, of philosophical interest. If it were a matter of pointing out that contemporary science as normally understood cannot accommodate any such view, and so we should be suspicious of it (as indeed we should of any view that contradicts or otherwise is at odds with the assumptions and findings of empirical science), then one would have no hesitation in sharing this worry; and it would be of philosophical interest. But there is nothing of this sort—nothing "unscientific" whether or not it is in fact true—in the idea that in being presented with certain emotions by music (or, if you like, in hearing certain sounds), a human being with such-and-such experiences and normal perceptual equipment will experience a certain kind of emotion (or feeling or mood or sensation) that has no object. In point of fact, objectless emotions, often blending into moods, are quite common and are provoked or occasioned by all sorts of things one experiences, whether by the outer senses or by inner imagination or by the food one eats. It is not clear to me whether or not, in saying that it is the beauty of the music that moves us, Kivy is also saying that the music or its beauty is the object of that feeling; it is not in general the case that the cause of an emotion, even when there is knowledge of that cause, makes it the object of the emotion. But the issue of the emotions and their objects is a large one and one that, lamentably, has rarely been considered as it really should be, that is, in the context of an ontology of the emotions itself embedded in a general ontological theory of the mind. I can only report that it seems to me, from my own experience, that my stirring from music is objectless even though I am aware of its cause. But in this case I will not presume to project my experience onto all humanity.

It seems odd to say that when a person is moved or stirred by *Le Sacre du Printemps* it is the beauty of the music that is responsible. The expression 'being moved' is, to be sure, sometimes limited in meaning to either a certain kind of feeling or a feeling with a particular kind of cause for which one is supposed to have a special respect and the existence of which in a person is supposed to reveal that person's sensitive nature and capacity for appreciation of music, at least of a certain kind. This form of being moved, or being moved by a certain kind of music, I suspect, just corresponds in a person with the disposition to describe certain pieces of music as beautiful and therefore also to suppose that it is the beauty of the music that really matters in the end and that explains most importantly why people listen to music.

If I am asked what it is about (the music of) *Le Sacre* that stirs me, I would reply: the rhythmic patterns especially in their repetitive aspects, the irregular meters of the final part, and *the like*. I might just say, in a casual manner, that it is an exciting piece of music, and while I might also say that the music is beautifully constructed or that Stravinsky has done a beautiful job of orchestration, and the like, I would never be tempted, at least spontaneously, to characterize the work as a beautiful piece of music, at least in the literal sense of being full of beauty. Why not, even though I admire and love the piece both as amateur composer and as listener? Do I take it to be unbeautiful or even ugly, as did many of its first listeners and, alas, as do some listeners in the late twentieth century, rejecting it as a piece they want to listen to or support being performed?

It is important to understand that we are not faced here with an ontological problem—that of the status of beauty in the sense of whether or not it is an "objective" property of some artworks and other objects and, if "objective," whether or not it is identical to some of the "natural" properties or instead different from any of them and, if different, whether or not it is "supervenient" on those "natural" properties, and so on. These issues, interesting and important as they may be, I have only once and then only briefly alluded to in this essay in order to distinguish my proper subject of *expressive* qualities from that of *evaluative* qualities (or, more precisely, *predicates*). For 'beautiful' is, above all, a predicate of evaluation or, as we might more commonly say in this context, of *taste*. And the issue before us is indeed not one of ontology, but instead one of musical culture and taste in music.

I submit that the emphasis on beauty in connection with artworks, and especially with musical artworks, is a symptom of the continuing domination of the contemporary culture of European-American art music by the music of the nineteenth century. From the way that performing musicians continue to be trained in music schools to the programming of nearly all major symphony orchestras to the repertories of nearly all opera companies, to the labeling of recordings by performer or conductor—in all these respects and others, our musical life is permeated by Romantic conceptions of "expressiveness" in music and the cult of the individual performing musician. The almost constant use of vibrato by string players—which is how they are trained!—is but one very obvious illustration of the custom (I hesitate to call it the application of a theory or a conscious choice among alternatives) of imposing a performance practice that originated in and is appropriate only to a certain kind of music that is typical of the nineteenth century—roughly what is known as Romantic music—onto all art music whether of the Baroque or other earlier times or of the Classical period or of our own century. One is required to be "expressive" at all costs! One must produce "beautiful" sounds and "beautiful" music, and that is music that best enables the performer (including the conductor) to "express" himself or herself.[4]

Kivy, the historian par excellence of the notion of expression in mu-

---

[4] This is exaggeration, to be sure, in order to make a point. Among necessary qualifications, we may take note most importantly of the "authenticity" movement in the performance of old music with its emphasis on (to use Peter Kivy's distinctions and words) "(1) faithfulness to the composer's performance intentions; (2) faithfulness to the performance practice of the composer's lifetime; (3) faithfulness to the sound of a performance during the composer's lifetime. . . . ," all of which lead away from emphasis on the performer's feelings. But Kivy notes that even in this context, "authenticity" sometimes also means "(4) faithfulness to the performer's own self, original, not derivative or aping of someone else's way of playing." Peter Kivy, *Authenticities: Philosophical Reflections of Musical Performance* (Ithaca: Cornell University Press, 1995), 6–7.

sic, has made clear to us the distinction between a broader use in which all or nearly all music is expressive and a narrower use in which the notion refers only to a certain kind of music of a certain culture; namely, Romantic art music of the European-American culture (*SS*, the chapter called "Representation as Expression"). What he may have failed to see is that the notion of beauty has an almost exactly parallel place: it can function to capture *whatever it is*, in any music, that moves a listener (or simply as another way of saying that one is "favorably" moved in some way or other), but it can also, and more commonly, function to indicate that one was moved by the music or its performance of a kind or manner that is typical of Romanticism.[5] That these should often be confused is only further evidence of the domination.

Is there anything to be learned from this continuing domination? Is there something about Romantic music and its atmosphere that teaches us something about ourselves or our culture? About ourselves, I would say it teaches us something only in the trivial sense that it shows us to be capable of a certain culture. As to the culture: despite the historical fact of the Stalinist endorsement of a late Romantic style in music, as exemplified by the "approved" music of Dmitri Shostakovich and Serge Prokofiev, it must be remembered that Romanticism in general, whether in music or painting or literature or even philosophy, is above all a celebration of the individual and more pointedly of the importance and value of individual "expression," whatever the demands and norms of society. Most contemporary artists, in all the arts, have been rendered incapable by our culture of even conceiving of art as anything more important than ways in which they express themselves.

It is the culture of a radical individualism, one that puts more value on the inner feeling than the outer product even in art, that sustains and is partly constituted by the continuing influence of Romanticism in our time.[6] To lament this influence is not in the least—especially in the

---

[5]   One can go even further in detecting a yet narrower sense in which the corresponding notions of "beauty" and "being moved" and perhaps of "expressiveness" are especially applicable to the music and a person's experience of it when it is a *slow* piece or movement or section of a piece of Romantic music.

[6]   This idea get its extreme philosophical expression in the thought of Leo Tolstoy and R. G. Collingwood, at least as they are often understood, in which the "real" art object is in the mind of the artist, while the painting or musical composition or other object usually thought of as the artwork is only the incidental public indication of the private mental events. See Tolstoy's *What Is Art?* (Indianapolis: Hackett, 1996) and Collingwood's *Principles of Art* (Oxford: Clarendon Press, 1938).

spirit of separating the product and its value from the person and that person's inner life—to denigrate the great achievements of Romanticism in any sphere, including music. Still, one can only long for the day when our musical culture is dominated by the music of our own time and in which the music of any time is performed in a manner appropriate to that music; and when musicians and listeners alike are liberated from the idea that, in doing music, the feelings of the musician are more important than those represented in the music that is being performed.

APPENDIX

A Look at the Literature

In this appendix I review some of the recent literature on representative theories of music, most of which takes the form of criticisms of Langer's theory. I first state and categorize the criticisms, then make some measure of reply to them, especially in the respects that are particularly pertinent to my own theory. But independent of my success in that endeavor, this appendix should help to make clearer just what those theories—Langer's and mine—maintain.

Let us start with Peter Kivy who, at least in his earlier writings, is one of the milder critics. He objects to Langer's idea that music is expressive (in whatever way) only of the *forms* of the emotions and not of their individual contents, citing common experience on his side (*SS*, 46). But he admits that arguments from the relativity of musical experience tend to support Langer, and he attempts to reply to those arguments (*SS*, 47–49). A little farther on (*SS*, 60), Kivy refers to "well-known objections" to Langer's theory. Without explicitly ascribing the error to Langer, he refers to the fallacy of going from "isomorphism" to "symbol," and, in this section devoted to distinguishing his views from hers, insists that this criticism does not apply to his theory. (He cites Ernest Nagel's review of *Philosophy in a New Key* and a book of Monroe Beardsley's as sources for identifying the fallacy.[1]) This objection to Langer I have

[1] Ernest Nagel, review of Langer's *Philosophy in a New Key*, *Journal of Philosophy* 40 (1943); and Monroe Beardsley, *Aesthetics: Problems in the Philosophy of Criticism* (New York: Harcourt, Brace, 1958).

already mentioned and, I believe, effectively answered on her behalf, but the issue itself—what makes the one *actually* about the other in the case of music and the emotions—is a further matter and, of course, one I have attempted to answer. The mildness of Kivy's criticisms derives from the fact that his own theory of this time is in many respects similar to Langer's, the crucial differences deriving from the fact that on his account, as I noted in chapter 6, it is the outward behavioral expressions of the emotions and not the emotions themselves or their physiological accompaniments that are directly represented (he doesn't like that word, however) by music.

Jerrold Levinson, who has a useful summary of Langer's theory in a footnote in his *Meaning, Art, and Metaphysics*, has several objections to what he calls "a Langerian hypothesis."[2] Three connected ones are stated in this way:

> One is the question of exactly what the structure or form of an emotion consists in. Another is the assumption that all instances of a given emotion in fact exhibit a common form or structure. A third is the assumption that the particular manner in which an emotion progresses is reasonably distinctive of it. (*MAM*, 283)

Levinson moves quickly on, however, to his main interest in mentioning the "Langerian hypothesis," to object that if only isomorphisms were relevant to what emotion is expressed, then *every* musical passage would be true, a consequence he deems unacceptable. Whether or not this conclusion is relevant to Langer's actual theory is dubious, but at any rate Levinson makes the substantive objection that what emotion is expressed by a given musical passage is, in fact, a function of many factors—including what emotions are aroused in the listener, what emotion the composer probably felt in composing it, what verbal and behavioral manifestations of emotion the music resembles, and more —and not *only* what emotion is "structurally mirrored" by the passage (*MAM*, 284). This suggests the idea I defended in the chapter 8 of there being multiple connections of music to the emotions. Levinson, however, wants at least many of these connections united in a single theory of "expression" and "truth" in music.

Another defender of "truth" in art is Wilson Coker, who, in his

---

[2] Jerrold Levinson, *Meaning, Art, and Metaphysics: Essays in Philosophical Aesthetics* (Ithaca: Cornell University Press, 1990), 282; *MAM* in the text.

Music and Meaning, berates Langer for failing to see that music is a "semiotic-gestural" system whose parts have truth values (correctly, I think, regarding her as denying that musical passages are either true or false). Citing philosophers Willard Van Orman Quine and Rudolph Carnap and composers Arnold Schoenberg and Milton Babbitt in his support, Coker characterizes theories like Langer's as "poppycock," at least if one accepts his semiotic-gestural theory.[3] The objection, in effect, is that Langer has not gone far enough in recognizing the symbolic nature of music; it really is even more like language than she realized.

Kathleen Higgins's useful discussion of Langer's views in her recent *The Music of Our Lives*, while favorable in some respects, suggests that Langer's account is overly intellectual and "ignores the possibility that music appeals primarily, or even importantly, to the emotions."[4] The objection seems to be that the theory is too cognitive, giving insufficient value or place for the actual experience of both music and the emotions. With respect to the isomorphism in Langer's account, Higgins raises a number of important issues. For one, Langer suggests both that physiological aspects of musical experience are irrelevant philosophically but that it is the physiological aspects of emotion with which music shares logical forms. To that extent (although perhaps depending on one's theory of the emotions themselves), Langer should not have said that music is a morphology of the emotions. Thus when Higgins asks whether or not "music provides patterns that are isomorphic with the full texture of the emotions," her reply is that "Langer does not demonstrate that it does" (*MOL*, 104).

But further, Higgins claims that Langer has not specified what she means by "musical patterns," those aspects of music that are said to be isomorphic with the emotions. Are they the patterns that, in Higgins's words, are "consciously observed by the listener" or instead those that are "analytically discovered" (*MOL*, 105), that is, that can, in the extreme cases, be discovered only by the trained musical theorist? This objection (perhaps one only of imprecision or incompleteness) touches on a general worry that, if I am not mistaken, lies behind some other objections: that it doesn't *seem* to us, at least not always as we listen to music, that we are being *presented with* the emotions by music, a

---

[3] Wilson Coker, *Music and Meaning: A Theoretical Introduction to Musical Aesthetics* (New York: Free Press, 1972), 137.

[4] Kathleen Higgins, *The Music of Our Lives* (Philadelphia: Temple University Press, 1991), 103; *MOL* in the text.

circumstance that Langer's theory seems to require. Higgins's own answer to the question is that for Langer it is probably "pattern observed" and not "pattern discovered" that is to be taken to be isomorphic with the emotions; but that, Higgins further objects, is something that is not so easily examined or specified (*MOL*, 105). In the end, however, Higgins somewhat praises Langer's "vagueness," albeit unintended, while criticizing her for using language, such as that of "isomorphism" and "unconsummated symbol," that suggests at least the possibility of a clarity and precision that is lacking and, Higgins suggests, must be lacking, given the nature of the subject matter (*MOL*, 105).

Roger Scruton, in his *Art and Imagination*, brings against Langer and other defenders of what he calls the "semantic theory" of expression the charge of triviality and emptiness.[5] The core of his criticism, directed most strongly against Nelson Goodman's theory of representation in *Languages of Art*, is that "reference to particulars," which he takes to be feature of both Langer's and Goodman's theories of art, presupposes the possibility of *translation*, for "reference to particulars cannot occur in a scheme of symbols that does not admit the possibility of predication, and hence the possibility of assigning truth-values" (*AI*, 224). Yet both Goodman and Langer deny, as they must, the possibility of translations of the symbolisms that, according to their respective theories, the arts are. All of this suggests to Scruton that "a semantic theory of art does not really say anything about appreciation that could not be said in less misleading terms" (*AI*, 225). As to his own account, which is not our business here, we may note only Scruton's insistence that it is as least misleading to think of the appreciation of art, including music, as *cognitive*; instead, he says, "symbolism in art is a matter of suggestion rather than reference" (*AI*, 226).

Malcolm Budd, whose purposes are, in the logical sense, mostly negative in his *Music and the Emotions*, is perhaps Langer's most severe and careful critic while at the same time providing what is probably the clearest and most detailed summary of her views to be found in the literature to date.[6] In his chapter devoted to her theory, titled "Music as Unconsummated Symbol," Budd raises a number of serious objections to the theory as stated by Langer, beginning with the reasonable sug-

[5] Roger Scruton, *Art and Imagination: A Study in the Philosophy of Mind* (London: Routledge and Kegan Paul, 1974), 221; *AI* in the text.
[6] Malcolm Budd, *Music and the Emotions: The Philosophical Theories* (London: Routledge and Kegan Paul, 1985); *ME* in the text.

gestion that Langer has not made as clear as desirable just what an un-consummated symbol is, by way of not making clear just what a symbol is. Appreciating, however, as some other critics have not, that Langer does provide an account of why music is symbolic of feelings and not the other way around (or both ways), Budd maintains that Langer's invocation of Wittgenstein for her notion of logical form (or structure or pattern) is unhelpful and hence that "her requirement that a discursive symbol should have the same structure as the 'object' it symbolises can-not be assessed" (*ME*, 111), the same presumably applying therefore to the presentational symbols of music, on her account.

In the second place, Budd objects that "there is no plausibility in the view that the present quality of our feelings has a structure that is incommensurable with that of any discursive symbol and that this structure can be more perfectly reflected by a presentational symbol" (*ME*, 112). In thus rejecting Langer's ineffability thesis, Budd believes that she has simply underestimated the power of language and claims that "there is no difficulty of principle in characterising precisely the particular nature of a feeling" (*ME*, 113). As a related point, Budd says that just because it is only the *forms* of feeling that, on Langer's theory, are symbolized by music, art cannot serve its presumed function, agreed to by Langer, of educating us in important ways if only because, ac-cording to Budd, "there appear to be no possibilities of this kind we are ignorant of and music could manifest to us" (*ME*, 113).

Yet another objection is based on the insistence that "neither is the class of emotions and feelings differentiated from all other classes by the kinds of forms they follow" (*ME*, 114). Hence, according to Budd, Langer has not really given us any reason to say that it is the emotions in particular that are symbolized by music as contrasted with any other things or processes that have those forms. (Here, possibly, Budd has momentarily forgotten that shared logical form is not, on Langer's ac-count, a sufficient condition for the symbolizing relation. But the objec-tion still makes the point of asking why, then, a composer could not symbolize something other than the emotions by music.) Nor, Budd claims, does Langer ever really argue for the proposition that "no part of the content of any feeling can be reflected in music" (*ME*, 115).

In a further objection, Budd calls attention to the fact that, unlike language, in which the symbols generally function only instrumentally in the sense of having no intrinsic interest to the speaker or listener, mu-sic as sound is just what the listener is primarily interested in. Hence,

Budd concludes, "it is not in general true for the listener that music is any kind of symbol" (*ME*, 116). This objection we may reasonably call the *phenomenological* one to any theory of music as representing or symbolizing something beyond itself. Further, Budd maintains, the theory provides no reason and even something of a counter-reason why we should find the music as heard something valuable and desirable (*ME*, 116) and, it would seem, why we should listen to the same piece of music repeatedly. Budd grants (*ME*, 117) that Langer's view that, in effect, we *forget* almost immediately after hearing a piece of music the details of what it symbolizes (while presumably retaining some lasting, beneficial effect) in some measure answers that objection, but denies that that is the *reason* anyone actually has for rehearing a piece of music. Furthermore, Budd notes, some simple pieces that we want to hear again can be remembered in their entirety (*ME*, 117).

Like Higgins, Budd raises the question of just what the structure of a piece of music is that is supposed to be isomorphic to the structure of the emotions, concluding that "if the structure of a musical work can be fitted to some form feeling is likely to follow this will only be in so general a manner as to omit most of the detail that gives the music its value" (*ME*, 118).

Finally, arising in part from the last-mentioned objection as well as some earlier-mentioned ones, Budd insists that Langer's theory "does not allow for the manifest possibility that different works have different musical values" (*ME*, 118). For if the value of a piece of music lies in its symbolizing function, then all one can say is that it symbolizes what it symbolizes; it cannot do it less well or better than some other piece of music unless—something that is excluded by the theory—one can specify in words independently just what form of feeling is being symbolized. Budd concludes that "the significance of music as an art-form cannot consist merely in music's being an unconsummated symbol" (*ME*, 118), contrary, it would seem, to Langer's guiding idea.

Stephen Davies devotes just over ten pages to Langer's theory in his recent *Musical Meaning and Expression*, most of it in either reporting or making criticisms of the theory.[7] Some of the objections, including his final one to the effect that the theory simply fails to explain why we are moved by music, derive from that curious feature of Langer's account according to which it is the *conceptions* of the emotions and not the emo-

---

[7]   *Musical Meaning and Expression*, 123–134.

tions themselves that are symbolized by music. (But she does also some-times say that it is the emotions themselves that are symbolized and other times that it is the outward expressions of the emotions that are isomorphic to music.) These objections we may safely ignore here, for my version of a representation theory has no such feature.

Davies also worries about the issue of "directionality" (how it is that music symbolizes the emotions instead of, or in addition to, the other way around), the issue of the theory of the emotions that Langer's the-ory is said to presuppose, and the issue of her theory's connection to the now allegedly discredited "picture" theory of meaning. But in the end, Davies' main if not sole firm objection to Langer's theory or any symbol theory of the "meaning" of music seems to be that a "possession" the-ory is a better explanation of the phenomena each purports to explain. These phenomena are: (1) the way we experience music in the sense of what we hear in it, and (2) the fact of our being moved by music. By a "possession" theory, Davies means one that locates in the music alone, and not in anything external to it, what explains its expressive qualities (or, more neutrally, that we apply the predicates of expression to music).

The foregoing constitutes, then, what I take to be the most important objections to Langer's theory specifically and, in many cases, to any rep-resentative theory of music.

In replying to and commenting on these objections, it will be useful to organize them under the headings of (a) the *logical* objections—those having to do with truth, reference, isomorphism, and the like; (b) the *empirical* objections—those having to do with the forms of music and the "forms" of the emotions; (c) the *content/expressive* objections—those having to do with what is expressed by music and its reception by the listener; (d) the *phenomenological* objections—those having to do with what people actually claim to hear and to be interested in in music; (e) the *desire/value* objections—those having to with what people desire from music and the values in it; and (6) the *best-explanation* objection—that having to do with, other objections aside, the proposition that the representative theory is the best explanation of what it tries to explain.

The logical objections

(1) *That isomorphism does not imply representation.* I most emphatically agree with this claim and have argued that, whatever be the case with Langer's theory, my theory offers, mainly in the notion of a quasi-

natural sign, independent and separate arguments for the thesis the music represents possible states of consciousness.

(2) *That the theory implies that all musical passages are true, which is contrary to fact.* This objection, I believe, confuses description with depiction, and it is just a mistake to suppose that any kind of symbolization implies that the symbols have truth values, painting being the most obvious and uncontroversial example.

(3) *That music* does *have truth values, contrary to Langer and other defenders of the representative theory.* The argument for truth values in music is based on assimilating its manner of symbolizing to that of language, which is a mistake. Insisting that all symbolism involves truth values is simply to blur the fundamental distinction between description and depiction or, to put it otherwise, between asserting and picturing.

(4) *That music cannot refer to anything because reference implies translatability, which music lacks.* This argument involves little more than an arbitrary stipulation on the use of the word *reference.* There is no substantive argument I know or can think of that would suggest that wherever in human experience one object symbolizes another, there must also be the possibility of "translating" the former into some other object that, in a systematic way, also symbolizes the latter. This is another argument that would too narrowly assimilate symbolism, wherever it exists, to that of language. And one could also wonder, for that matter, if even in the case of language itself such translatability is a necessary condition for reference. As in all such cases, the answer may depend on the sense of the modal term.

(5) *That music is isomorphic to other things and processes besides emotions and other conscious states, making those other things and processes equally plausible candidates for what music would represent, if it represented anything.* This is really but another version of the "isomorphism doesn't imply representation" objection, so the same reply—that separate arguments need to be made and have been made for the thesis that music does represent certain states of consciousness and not other things—is appropriate. To this may be added that while the kinds of conscious states that are represented by music may go beyond the emotions, the anthropological fact is that it is primarily the predicates of the emotions and not of other (nonmusical) things and events that are applied to music.

(6) *That the idea of shared logical form or isomorphism is incoherent or at least not entirely clear.* Isomorphism is undoubtedly a murky notion as applied to music and the mind. I have tried to clarify it somewhat in the

analysis of the ontological affinity between consciousness and sound and in other ways. One hopes that the future will bring further enlightenment on the nature of the connection, if there really is one, between music and certain states of consciousness. This *is* the ontological heart of the matter, and I take my most important contribution to be to have exposed that heart while admittedly not yet making fully clear how it works in detail.

(7) *That language is, in fact, equipped to describe any aspect of emotion, which fact denies to music an important function that the representative theory ascribes to and purports partly to explain.* As we know, the ineffability thesis is, in fact, logically independent of the representative theory, for the thesis that music can depict some things that language cannot describe (or, better put, can capture some *differences* in mental life that language cannot capture) depends on a thesis about language as well. I have made my case that language cannot, even in principle, capture every difference of mood and feeling that can or does exist in reality. That, of course, does not prove that music or anything else can do what language cannot do, but it does leave open the possibility, which is all that this criticism was intent on disproving.

The empirical objections

(8) *That it is unclear just what the form of an emotion is, the form being what is supposed to be represented by music.* In point of fact, I think Langer virtually identified the form of an emotion with its physiological accompaniments (to whatever extent that observation may be helpful). My theory, in any case, is not based on the notion of the identity or similarity of the forms (although there may be such) of music and the emotions but on the somewhat looser yet more plausible idea that the form and the content of music combine to represent the emotions and other states of consciousness in their forms and contents, however exactly those might be characterized. It is more that a passage of music *as a whole* represents a state of consciousness or, better, a series of configurations of states of consciousness, also *as a whole*.

(9) *That the same emotion can have different forms under different circumstances.* This fact, if it is a fact, would not contradict the possibility that a given piece or passage of music represents a given emotion in one of its putatively multiple forms. But, as just indicated, and agreeing with Kivy and others that both the forms and the contents of the emotions

are expressed (whatever that comes to) by music, my theory is not one that is restricted in either representative or represented as to the forms of the objects involved.

(10) *That the form of an emotion is not what makes it the emotion it is.* Langer was in full agreement with this claim and used it to account for the ambiguity in music and for differences of judgment among knowledgeable listeners about what the music expresses. This was based, ultimately, if I am not mistaken, on the fact that very different but equally intense emotions can have very similar and at least partly identical bodily and behavioral accompaniments and expressions. But if one holds that it is the contents as well as the forms of the emotions that are represented by music and also that it is primarily the emotions themselves and not their physiological and behavioral accompaniments that are represented, then the fact that there is more to an emotion's being the emotion it is than its form is consistent with, and accommodated by, the new theory.

(11) *That while she says that it is the emotions themselves that are represented by music, Langer's examples make it clear that it is really only their physiological accompaniments that are represented, if anything is.* I think that this is a just criticism of Langer's theory as she states it, which statement reflects her lack of clarity on the nature of the emotions themselves. And I believe that this lack of clarity itself derives from a deeper and, in my judgment, unsolvable problem that she shares with many other philosophers: how to accommodate the richness of the "inner" life within an essentially materialist ontology. Because my theory recognizes the distinctness of the emotions from their physiological accompaniments (and the distinctness generally of conscious states from their bodily causes, effects, and expressions), and maintains explicitly that it is the emotions themselves (or, even more precisely, the *havings* of emotions) that are represented by music, it is immune to this criticism.

(12) *That it is unclear what the form of a piece of music is that is supposed to represent—in particular, whether it is the form of the music heard by the listening to it or the form discovered upon analysis (where those differ).* This *may* be a fair criticism of Langer's theory, but on mine this distinction loses much of its relevance insofar as on the new theory, with its distinction between attentive awareness on the one side and inattentive awareness and nonattentive awareness on the other, all that is required is that what is given to a person by auditory means, whether or not it involves attentive awareness of those aspects of the music, is what is or may be

involved in the representation by the music. Any property of the music that, in principle, cannot be given to the hearing obviously cannot be playing a relevant role (it may have an extraneous causal role, as anything might) in the representation. But here one must be careful. Probably no one can tell, just by listening, that, for example, a given section of a piece of music is exactly twice as long in performance time as the immediately preceding section; but the fact that it is so is given to one all the same and may, therefore, play a role in the nature of the representation involved. There will ordinarily be attentive awareness of the music as such, needless to say, but there will also ordinarily be either inattentive awareness or nonattentive awareness of many of the music's particular properties, and any of these may play a role in the quasi-natural representation that permits the nonattentive awareness of certain states of consciousness.

(13) *That what gives music its distinctive character and its value is independent of, and perhaps even contradictory of, the idea that is isomorphic to the emotions.* This criticism is somewhat reminiscent of Kivy's point in his *Pure Music* that I discussed in chapter 6, and to the extent that this objection forces one to stress that a listener's pleasure in, and the value one assigns to, the music must derive from *its* properties, one may agree with it. At the same time, however, one must insist, in the absence of any argument to the contrary, first, that these facts in no way diminish, much less contradict, the possibility that music also represents the emotions and other states of consciousness, and, second, that some of the properties of the music itself in which we do take pleasure and find value may also, by allowing the music to represent something that is not music, help to explain our natural impulse to label some of those properties of the music as we do.

The content/expressive objections

(14) *That it is not only the form but both the form and the content of the emotions that are expressed in music, whatever expression amounts to.* With this objection to Langer's theory I agree, and the new theory embodies the thesis that Langer's denies. But to the extent that this fact is advanced as showing that expression in music cannot be, or be dependent on, representation by music, it remains to be shown, as I believe it cannot be shown, that music cannot represent the contents as well as the forms of certain states of consciousness.

(15) *That whatever emotion is expressed by a particular piece of music is a function of many factors and not only, if at all, that of what the music represents.* The new theory is about what music represents, and in agreeing that there may sometimes, perhaps always, be other connections of the music to the emotions (in addition to that of representation) that jointly go into what the music "expresses" (as I did agree and even insist in chapter 8), one can also agree that, as it were, expression is more than representation. But that needn't cast any doubt on the proposition that expression is *at least* representation. And that is what the new theory requires.

(16) *That music appeals primarily to the emotions and not, as the representative theory implies, to the intellect.* This objection is not easy to assess in a few words. Part of the appeal of art is just its *joint* appeal to the emotions and the intellect, and surely both do play important roles in serious listening to music. Whatever Langer may have held about the matter, there would seem to be nothing in a representative theory as such that implies anything about the kinds or the proportions of the kinds of appeal that music has for human beings. Rembrandt's self-portraits depict Rembrandt: does that imply that the appeal in perceiving or even studying one of them is primarily intellectual? Surely not. Furthermore, the distinction between appeal to the intellect and appeal to the emotions is, especially in the case of the appreciation of art, of dubious significance at least in the sense that either may be a reason for indulging the other: the emotional impact of a Rembrandt self-portrait may be cause for coming to study and understand and admire how that effect was achieved, which in turn may intensify and widen the emotional consequences. One may well recall, in this different context from that about which he wrote, Hume's famous dictum about "reason" and the "passions." As to the general issue of emotion *from* music (as contrasted with emotion "*in*" music), I had my say in the final chapter.

(17) *That the appreciation of symbolism in music is a matter of suggestion and not of cognitive processes, as the representative theory implies.* The representative theory, especially in the form that I have developed of it, does indeed imply that there are processes of awareness and understanding in the listening to music of a sort reasonably called cognitive at the heart of the phenomenon of symbolism in music. But this is, once again, not to deny the *multiple* ways that music, somewhat like paintings that unquestionably depict something, has its effects on us, whatever

might reasonably be meant by "appreciating the symbolism through suggestion." I shall only mention again the artificiality of this somewhat similar distinction to that of the immediately preceding objection, but I want to say that just as the representative theory merely as a representative theory implies almost nothing about what else may occur in the listening to music, so does whatever else may occur imply little about the possibility of representation in music. What else does occur *may* have implications for the *probability* of such representation, especially if it can be shown that their occurrence is a better or even equally good explanation of what, according to the defenders of the representative theory, it best explains.

The phenomenological and desire/value objections

(18) *That we don't seem to be presented with the emotions (or their forms or their physiological accompaniments) or anything else in listening to music.* I have dealt with this objection at great length in earlier chapters, mainly by invoking the notion of nonattentive awareness.

(19) *That music is not a symbol, at least in any way like language, for it is the music itself we are interested in and not what it purportedly represents, unlike the analogous situation with language.* I have also dealt with this objection in considerable measure, partly by suggesting that art just is the realm of human experience in which, above all if not uniquely, one is interested in *both* the artwork and what, if anything, it symbolizes. This objection to representation in music would suggest that there is no symbolism in any of the arts—no representation or depiction or picturing—at least to whatever extent it is the artwork itself that commands our interest. And that is absurd.

(20) *That the representative theory makes it hard to understand why we are ever disposed to listen to the same piece of music again.* Langer's unfortunate answer to this objection is that we forget what was presented to us by a piece of music shortly after hearing it. I do not wish to argue whether or not this is true (it seems clearly false to the extent that one can "go through" the music in one's head, as we say) because the best answer to the objection is again to point to other arts in which, where there is undoubted representation and indeed "essential" representation (as in literature), we nonetheless return to the same artwork repeatedly. This phenomenon has whatever mystery it does have, but there can be no

doubt about its occurrence and therefore no grounds for doubt about representation in music because of the mystery of our return to the same piece of music.

(21) *That because we cannot say to what degree a composer succeeded in symbolizing certain states of consciousness, we cannot assign different values to different pieces of music, which is absurd.* This objection presupposes a principle of evaluation of artworks including music that is to be rejected. The principle is that the value of a piece of music, and any artwork, is a function of the distance between the artist's intention and the artist's success in realizing that intention in the artwork—the smaller the distance, the greater the value. While there are contexts in which we feel called upon to praise a work in mind of its creator's age or training (or, in these days, sex or race or species or whatever), in general we not only should but even "must" make an evaluation of the artwork independent of how it came about in order to assess to what extent the artist may have succeeded in achieving, in the artwork itself, what he or she (or it) set out to achieve. And the same goes in all fields of human endeavor. By "must" I mean only that in raising, if one chooses to do so, the question of what the distance is between intention and achievement, one is guided by an assessment of the value of the achievement in itself. One would not suppose that I have produced a great work of literature in the prosework that consists entirely of the words "Books are" because I can truthfully report that my achievement fully realized my intentions; one would be interested in neither intention nor achievement just because the achievement, in itself, is of no value. Effort, sincerity, strong motive, rich intentions, and much more about artists and humans generally are themselves of value, but they do not, in general, confer value on their external consequences merely by being the causes of those consequences, whatever they are.

The representative theory is again therefore being ascribed a consequence (in the logical sense) that it does not have. It is true that Langer, unfortunately, sometimes writes as if composers were consciously trying to represent the emotions in their music *and*, what is separate, that great music is that music in which composers succeed in these attempts. This is not an unnatural way to talk about the creation of artworks, but it is ultimately misleading. My theory, as I have suggested earlier, of representation in music has *nothing* to do, analytically speaking, with the intentions of composers: the music symbolizes what it does symbolize however it came about. Nor does my theory in itself have any implications for judgments of the value of a given piece of music, although I have no reluctance to agreeing that the nature of the actual representation that occurs in the music, whatever was intended, is highly relevant to the evaluation of the music. And that does not require that we be able independently to characterize the emotions that the music represents in order to assess the success of the composer, intentionally or not, in representing them.

The best-explanation objection

This objection I have already dealt with at length in chapter 8, and have nothing to add here.

It thus seems that the new theory is either immune to, or can effectively deflect, the criticisms that have been made both specifically of Langer's theory but also, in some cases, of any representative theory. Are there objections to be made of the new theory in the respects in which it differs from, and goes beyond, Langer's theory? I can think of none that have not already been dealt with, although there are undoubtedly, as with any theory of any significance, at least a few rough edges of both meaning and argument. The intrinsic plausibility of a theory lies in the nature of the available evidence and arguments for and against it as compared with extant competing theories for what it would describe and explain. Thus my own degree of confidence in the new theory is irrelevant, but I do submit that the case has been made for the proposition that it is the best theory for accounting for the most important connection between music and the emotions.

References

Addis, Laird. "Pains and Other Secondary Mental Entities." *Philosophy and Phenomenological Research* 47 (1986): 59–74.

———. "Dispositional Mental States: Chomsky and Freud." *Zeitschrift für Allgemeine Wissenschaftstheorie* 19 (1988): 1–17.

———. *Natural Signs: A Theory of Intentionality*. Philadelphia: Temple University Press, 1989.

———. "The Ontology of Emotion." *Southern Journal of Philosophy* 33 (1995): 261–278.

Beardsley, Monroe. *Aesthetics: Problems in the Philosophy of Criticism*. New York: Harcourt, Brace, 1958.

Bergson, Henri. *Time and Free Will*. 1910. Translated by F. L. Pogson. New York: Harper Torchbooks, 1960.

Budd, Malcolm. *Music and the Emotions: The Philosophical Theories*. London: Routledge and Kegan Paul, 1985.

Coker, Wilson. *Music and Meaning: A Theoretical Introduction to Musical Aesthetics*. New York: Free Press, 1972.

Collingwood, R. G. *The Principles of Art*. Oxford: Clarendon Press, 1938.

Davies, Stephen. *Musical Meaning and Expression*. Ithaca: Cornell University Press, 1994.

Durkheim, Emile. *The Elementary Forms of the Religious Life*. 1915. Translated by Joseph Ward Swain. New York: Free Press, 1965.

Frege, Gottlob. "On Sense and Reference." 1892. In *Translations from the Philosophical Writings of Gottlob Frege*, by Peter Geach and Max Black. Oxford: Basil Blackwell, 1960.

Freud, Sigmund. *On Dreams*. 1901. Translated by James Strachey. New York: W. W. Norton, 1952.

———. *Civilization and Its Discontents*. 1930. Translated by Joan Riviere. New York: Doubleday Anchor Books, 1958.

———. *On the Interpretation of Dreams*. 1900. Translated by James Strachey. New York: Avon Books, 1965.

Goodman, Nelson. *Languages of Art: An Approach to a Theory of Symbols*. Indianapolis: Hackett, 1976.

Grünbaum, Adolf. *Validation in the Clinical Theory of Psychoanalysis: A Study in the Philosophy of Psychoanalysis*. Madison: International Universities Press, 1993.

Hanslick, Eduard. *The Beautiful in Music*. 1854. Translated by Gustav Cohen from the seventh German edition on 1891. New York: Liberal Arts Press, 1957.

Higgins, Kathleen. *The Music of Our Lives*. Philadelphia: Temple University Press, 1991.

Hiller, Johann. "Abhandlung von der Nachahmung der Natur in der Musik." *Historisch-kritische Beyträge*, edited by Friedrich Wilhelm Marpurg, vol. 1, Berlin 1 (1754): 515–543.

Jacquette, Dale, *Philosophy of Mind*. Englewood Cliffs: Prentice Hall, 1994.

Jaynes, Julian. *The Origin of Consciousness in the Breakdown of the Bicameral Mind*. Boston: Houghton Mifflin, 1976.

Kivy, Peter. *The Corded Shell: Reflections on Musical Expression*. Princeton: Princeton University Press, 1980.

———. *Sound and Semblance: Reflections on Musical Representation*. Princeton: Princeton University Press, 1984.

———. *Sound Sentiment: An Essay on the Musical Emotions*. Philadelphia: Temple University Press, 1989.

———. *Music Alone: Philosophical Reflections on the Purely Musical Experience*. Ithaca: Cornell University Press, 1990.

———. *The Fine Art of Repetition: Essays in the Philosophy of Music*. Cambridge: Cambridge University Press, 1993.

———. *Authenticities: Philosophical Reflections on Musical Performance*. Ithaca: Cornell University Press, 1995.

———. *Philosophies of Art: An Essay in Differences*. Cambridge: Cambridge University Press, 1997.

Langer, Susanne. *Philosophy in a New Key: A Study in the Symbolism of Reason, Rite, and Art*. 1942. Third Edition. Cambridge: Harvard University Press, 1951.

———. *Feeling and Form: A Theory of Art*. New York: Charles Scribner's Sons, 1953.

Levinson, Jerrold. *Meaning, Art, and Metaphysics: Essays in Philosophical Aesthetics*. Ithaca: Cornell University Press, 1990.

Mew, Peter. "The Expression of Emotion in Music." *British Journal of Aesthetics* 25 (1985): 33–42.

Meyer, Leonard. *Emotion and Meaning in Music*. Chicago: University of Chicago Press, 1956.

Moore, G. E. "The Subject Matter of Psychology." *Proceedings of the Aristotelian Society* 10 (1910): 36–62.

Nagel, Ernest. Review of Langer's *Philosophy in a New Key. Journal of Philosophy* 40 (1943): 323–329.

Putnam, Hilary. *Reason, Truth and History.* Cambridge: Cambridge University Press, 1981.

Raffman, Diana. *Language, Music, and the Mind.* Cambridge: MIT Press, 1993.

Ridley, Aaron. *Music, Value and the Passions.* Ithaca: Cornell University Press, 1995.

Russell, Bertrand. *Philosophy.* New York: W. W. Norton, 1927.

——. "Knowledge by Acquaintance and Knowledge by Description." 1911. In his *Mysticism and Logic and Other Essays.* Totowa, N.J.: Barnes and Noble, 1981.

Sartre, Jean-Paul. *Being and Nothingness: An Essay on Phenomenological Ontology.* 1943. Translated by Hazel E. Barnes. New York: Washington Square Press, 1966.

Scruton, Roger. *Art and Imagination: A Study in the Philosophy of Mind.* London: Routledge and Kegan Paul, 1974.

Storr, Anthony. *Music and the Mind.* New York: Free Press, 1992.

Strawson, P. F. *Individuals: An Essay in Descriptive Metaphysics.* 1959. New York: Anchor Books, 1963.

Tolstoy, Leo. *What is Art?* 1896. Translated by Aylmer Maude. Indianapolis: Hackett, 1996.

Wittgenstein, Ludwig. *Tractatus Logico-Philosophicus.* Translated by C. K Ogden. London: Routledge and Kegan Paul, 1922.

——. *Philosophical Investigations.* Translated by G. E. M. Anscombe. Oxford: Basil Blackwell, 1953.

Zuckerhandl, Victor. *Sound and Symbol: Music and the External World.* Translated by Willard R. Trask. New York: Pantheon, 1956.

Index